LUTHERAN
HIGH SCHOOL
RELIGION SERIES ®

One Body in Christ

A Study of the Church

Teacher's Guide for Grade 10

By James Klawiter

Edited by Board for Parish Services Staff
Editor: Arnold E. Schmidt
Editorial Secretary: Phoebe Wellman

CONCORDIA

Publishing House
St. Louis

Contents

Unit 6: Conflict and Victory

To the Teacher

One Body in Christ, designed for tenth-grade students, provides an overview of the church, especially as presented in the epistles of St. Paul (primarily Ephesians and 1 and 2 Timothy). Students will learn about blessings God gives them through the church and of ways they can respond to God's love to build up one another within the church and to demonstrate His love through the church to those outside the church.

This course may be taught (with adaptations) also in grades 9, 11, or 12.

One Body in Christ is a 45-session course, providing resources for half of one semester. We recommend class five days per week. However, if the class meets less often, you might (a) extend the material in this course over a longer period of time, (b) assign certain sessions to individuals or small groups for reports in class, or (c) select sessions or units in accordance with class periods available.

THE LUTHERAN HIGH SCHOOL RELIGION SERIES

This is one of 12 courses for Lutheran high schools. The courses have been designed for a variety of scheduling programs. Four courses contain 90 sessions each and provide materials for five sessions per week for one semester. Each of the other eight courses contains 45 sessions and is designed for one quarter (half a semester).

Following are the topics of the 12 courses:

Grade 9
Interpersonal relationships (45 sessions)
Jesus' teachings from the Gospel of John (45 sessions)
Old Testament history (90 sessions)

Grade 10
New Testament history—including early church history (90 sessions)
The church in Paul's epistles (45 sessions)
Christian ethics (45 sessions)

Grade 11
Christian doctrine (90 sessions)
Later church history: Luther and the Reformation; Lutheranism (45 sessions)
Christian and non-Christian religions and cults (45 sessions)

Grade 12
Personal Christian living (90 sessions)
Engagement and marriage (45 sessions)
The general epistles and Revelation (45 sessions)

This design was prepared after a survey of all high schools affiliated with the Association for Lutheran Secondary Schools and after extensive conversations with high school and college teachers. Thus, it reflects both current practices and theory. The Parish Services staff wishes to express a special word of thanks to the ALSS administrators for their cooperation and assistance.

While any course assumes a certain background and maturity of the students, each course can stand alone—a previous course in this series is not an *absolute* prerequisite. The Student Books contain no grade-level designations; therefore courses can be adapted to other grade levels.

MATERIALS

In addition to this guide, you will need a copy of the accompanying Student Book and a Bible. (This course generally quotes the New International Version of the Bible. We recommend that you select a translation commonly used in the congregations of your students.)

The students will need a copy of the Student Book and a Bible. They will also need access to other resources, such as Bible dictionaries and concordances.

USING THIS GUIDE

Some sessions suggest more activities than can be accomplished in one period. Be selective. You know your students. Use the activities and materials that will be of most value to them.

LAW AND GOSPEL

The plans in this guide help you structure sessions so that students see both Law and Gospel. You will want the Holy Spirit to work in them as they hear God's words of accusation, forgiveness, and guidance. As you begin to plan the course, you might reread *The Proper Distinction Between Law and Gospel* by C. F. W. Walther. This is good reading for all who work with youth, especially teachers.

Once (**John 12:20—21**) some Greeks came to Philip and said, **"Sir, we would like to see Jesus."** Your basic goal as you teach each day should be to bring students to "see Jesus." Confront them with their spiritual needs; then lead them to see Jesus their Savior as the Answer to those needs. Let His love permeate all relationships in your classroom as you grow together in grace by the Spirit's power. Set this as your primary goal, and let all other objectives grow within this goal.

We invite you to write the editors about *One Body in Christ*. Share the joys and frustrations you experienced as you taught this course, offer suggestions for other courses, etc. Please send your comments to

Editorial Services Unit
Board for Parish Services
The Lutheran Church—Missouri Synod
1333 South Kirkwood Road
St. Louis, MO 63122-7295

A NOTE FROM THE AUTHOR

Many 10th-graders think of the church as an organization they "have gone to," perhaps have "become members of;" and possibly "enjoy going to Youth Group at." Others may never have had anything to do with the church. At any rate, a study of the church in St. Paul's Epistles would not be high on their list of topics to study.

This course has been designed to counteract this attitude. With God's blessings students will recognize that the church is a vital part of their lives, and they are a vital part of the church. They will be able to tell about the blessings they receive from God through the church and about the opportunities that exist within the church for them to respond to God's love, thus building up others within and outside the church.

Having friends and belonging is a big item with 10th graders. Therefore they should be ready to leave a juvenile, self-centered view of faith and move toward the concept of being a part of "the community of believers."

This course has been designed to enlarge teenagers' areas of spiritual concern beyond themselves. Through a study of Paul's writings about the church, they will be led to see that, as members of the church, they are the concern of other Christians and other Christians should be their concern.

TERMINOLOGY

Since the terms "believers" and "Christians" may seem like little more than cliches to many young people, we use the term "called-out ones" to refer to members of this body of Christ. We became Christians--we believe in the Lord Jesus as our Savior--because we have been "called out" by God. This term puts the emphasis and credit where it should be--on God. He is the One who has been active in us. He has made us members of His church.

OBJECTIVES

As you prepare to teach this course, keep in mind these **teacher objectives** for yourself. With God's power and blessing you will

1. present the Good News of salvation in every lesson by word and example;

2. establish a classroom climate that encourages serious Bible study, enjoyable discussion, freedom to question, and support for spiritual growth;

3. use the Bible as the basis for all discussion in regards to doctrine and practice, using both Law and Gospel;

4. demonstrate that life in the church is an enjoyable experience, a challenge, and a privilege;

5. use this text as a tool, not a master.

Following are some **student objectives** to observe and encourage as the course progresses. Through the power of the Holy Spirit the students will

1. become more sure of salvation through Christ;
2. give evidence of growing concern for one another as members of the church;
3. become more adept and comfortable in witnessing their faith in and out of class;
4. become more appreciative of the gifts of the Spirit through the church;
5. become effective members of a local congregation and leaders in the church.

ADVANCE PREPARATIONS

Some of the suggested activities in this course require long-range preparation:

Session 3: A collection of newspapers and magazines that reflect the unbelieving, unfruitful life

Session 15: Hymnals and/or other worship materials for a class worship service

Session 17: An outside speaker

Session 25: A current list of missionary addresses

Session 39: A collection of news items or church ads that demonstrate how people are misled by fake promises

Session 44: Resources to conduct a concluding worship activity (and perhaps a party)

COMPONENTS

The sessions in this course follow an organizational pattern designed to capture the attention of 10th-graders. This pattern follows the framework of an athletic event. Each session contains:

1. a section to get students into the topic;
2. a study of what God's Word says about the topic;
3. a reinforcement or practice activity.

The titles of these sections change as the course progresses as follows:

Units 1-20:
1. Stretching
2. Getting the Word

3. Practice

Units 21-40:
1. Warm-Up
2. First Half
3. Second Half

Units 41-45:
1. Final Whistle
2. Celebration
3. Celebration

Each session also contains suggestions for a devotional activity. These have been placed at the end of the session. Since they are not mentioned in the Student Book, you can use them at any time. As you plan your sessions, evaluate the appropriateness of using prayer or devotion to "calm things down" at the beginning of the session. A devotion at the end of the lesson may help students truly focus on what God has done and to thank Him accordingly. Various ideas are suggested. They are designated as "Wrap-Up" in Session 1-40 and "Final Worship" in Sessions 41-43.

Finally, each session ends with a verse from Scripture. Its purpose is twofold:

1. To summarize the main point of each session.
2. To provide content for a memorization course. Many high-school theology instructors include such a requirement and find that teenagers memorize remarkably well. In fact, many take pride in doing so. One rationale for encouraging memorization is: "The only Bible we have is the one we know." Memorization is not mentioned in the Student Book. Therefore this activity is optional.

TEACHING HINTS

Central Truth and Objectives

Be sure you have a clear picture of where your lesson is going and what you hope to see when you get there. The Central Truth summarizes where you are going. Objectives tell what you hope to accomplish.

Bible Basis

Each session serves as a vehicle to bring God and your students together.

Therefore the Bible texts are crucial. We generally present a plan to study larger texts in context and in depth, rather than studying all the associated passages. This method will enable students to study how the church is presented in the writings of St. Paul, especially **Ephesians** and **1 and 2 Timothy**.

Getting into the Topic ("Stretching," "Warm-Up," or "Final Whistle")

Use this section to motivate students--to stimulate them to think about the topic. Move quickly through this section. At times you may want to omit it entirely.

A Study of God's Word ("Getting the Word," "First Half," or "Celebration")

This is the main part of the entire session, for here God speaks directly through the text. This guide provides detailed procedures and suggestions. Do not feel bound to follow every suggestion. Rather, use your skill as a teacher to adapt the suggestions to fit your situation and your students. As you do, consider these ideas:

1. Many class activities will proceed more smoothly if all students use the same Bible translation. The Student Book uses the New International Version. You may, however, choose another translation. Consider translations used in other classes in your school and in the congregations in your area as you make your decision.

2. While both preaching and teaching can be effective means to impart religious knowledge, we suggest that you follow the teaching mode for these classes. The format of both the Student Book and this guide assumes that each class period will contain many opportunities of teacher-student and student-student interaction.

3. Take time to prepare adequately for each session. Be sure to have a clear idea of where each lesson is going and how to get there. Read the Bible and student texts and evaluate the answers suggested in this guide. Remember, as the instructor you make the final decision about what should happen in your classroom.

4. Pray. Tap into the power that the Holy Spirit provides. Ask each day that He use you to bring His thoughts to the lives of your students.

Reinforcement or Practice ("Practice," "Second Half," or "Celebration")

Each session should include some individual or group practice. We suggest a variety of devices and activities. Some can be accomplished better individually; others in groups. Since one of the course goals is to establish a sense of community, be sure to do some group work regularly.

Left on their own, 10th graders may talk a lot in groups, but the talking may not accomplish a task or arrive at a conclusion. Therefore you will need to teach skills of group work. For example:

1. Select groupings yourself-- friends do not always work well together.

2. Have two or three students in each group. More may create the "boss" and the "mouse in the corner."

3. Designate a leader or recorder-- someone to lead and be responsible to report to the class or to you.

4. Establish a definite, reachable goal. Also establish some way students can demonstrate this goal.

5. Allow each group "breathing room." That is, do not impose your thoughts on them. Be available to explain, encourage, and correct (get them back on the track), but do not become "a teacher in the group."

6. Encourage openness and honesty without fear or ridicule. (Tenth-graders can be cruel in their reactions.) Use group work to practice being the church, to support, and to confirm one another.

When doing individual work, make sure each student does his or her own thinking. Use individual work on the easier and more obvious activities.

On occasion, work together as a class. This provides the opportunity for instant verification of correct or incorrect thinking. Use whole class work on the more difficult activities.

It is the prayer of the author and editors that our Lord will use this course to help you and your students develop a closer relationship with Him and a more effective role in His church.

Unit 1: What the Church Is

One of the burdens of the English language is having one word serve more than one purpose. Such a word is *church.* Your students have used this word ever since they have been old enough to talk. And now as "almost adults" their concept of the church is no doubt centered in an organization, a building, or in a combination of both.

This introductory unit should help them clarify the term. We will look at the church as the gathering of "called-out ones." The emphasis is on the One who called them into membership and gives them the spiritual strength they need to believe what the Gospel tells them. With His blessing we become a part of this church.

By the end of the unit your class should recognize that they are involved in more than a congregation, a building, or a class. They should see themselves as an important part of God's eternal plan.

Session 1: God Created It

BIBLE BASIS: Eph. 1

CENTRAL TRUTH

God ordained the formation of the church by calling out those whom He had chosen for salvation. In time He gathers them together as His church, with Christ as its Head.

OBJECTIVES

That the students will

1. define the church as the community of "called-out ones";

2. list the steps God used in forming His church;

3. explain that church membership is entirely God's work of grace;

4. describe their own personal history of church membership;

5. express confidence in God's **continued care for their spiritual well-being.**

BACKGROUND

The church did not come into being as a result of human scheming. No, God caused its birth. Note the words in *Eph. 1* that refer to Him as the One who is responsible for the creation of the church: *Chose* (**v. 4**), *predestined . . . His pleasure and will* (**v. 5**), *purposed* (**v. 9**), *chosen . . . predestined . . . purpose of His will* (**v. 11**), *hope to which He has called you* (**v. 18**), etc.

To make this point--that *God* created the church and is responsible for the blessings we enjoy in it-- emphasize the study of **verses 3-14.** Be sure, though, to also allow time to personalize the study. Students should realize, "God chose *me!* I'm important to Him! I'm a part of His church, of His body!"

See **"Components"** in the introduction to this guide for discussion about the way each session is organized.

Pray that the Holy Spirit will use you to bring rich spiritual growth to your students during this course.

STRETCHING (Objective 1)

Have the students read this introductory story silently. Then ask volunteers to tell about times when they were included in special groups. Dwell on the feelings they experienced when this happened. Make the transition to the reading in **Ephesians.**

GETTING THE WORD (Objectives 2-3, and 5)

Following are some suggestions about Bible reading in the 10th grade:

1. Many 10th-graders do not like to read orally, so don't insist on it. Others take pride in this ability; use them instead.

2. If possible, use the same translation so all may follow along easily.

3. Vary your Bible reading practices. For example:

a. Use one reader per section.

b. Do the reading yourself, especially if it contains difficult words.

c. Have students read silently, especially if they are using several translations.

d. Have each student read a paragraph or a verse.

e. Listen to a recording of the passage.

Whatever you do, make the use of Scripture in your classroom as interesting as possible.

Verses 1-2

This is the usual form for the greeting in the epistles: name of author; name of addressee; a list of some spiritual blessings.

Be sure to discuss the four individuals named here. You might want to read **Gal. 1:1—2:10** for additional information about Paul's start as an apostle.

In connection with "the saints in Ephesus," some older manuscripts do not include "in Ephesus." (The letter may have been written to several churches, including the one at Ephesus.) You may not want to discuss this issue, however, since the emphasis here is on "saints." Be sure to emphasize the definition of "saints" as given.

Verses 3-14

1. Paul used the first person plural for those who are redeemed. Salvation is based on God's activity, not on ours.

2. The difference between the two lists should be quite obvious. Be sure to point out that our salvation does not depend on our personal feelings or activity, but solely on God's actions. All of us are equal—we all became members of God's church in the same way.

3. The first column in the Student Book outlines God's activity for us:

a. *Blessed us* (**v. 3**)—a term that summarizes all of God's work for us.

b. *Chose us* (**v. 4**)—a conscious act of grace on God's part. Human logic suggests an inverse to this act—that God then chose some people for damnation. But God's logic goes beyond human logic. He wants all to be saved, and does not choose that anyone be damned. (You may want to avoid that whole issue at this time so you can focus on the joy and comfort we receive from the knowledge that God has chosen us.)

c. *Predestined us* (**v. 5**). This term does not mean we are "locked in." It does show God's conscious love for us in choosing us from eternity to be saved. Think of predestination as God knowing that our final destination is heaven.

d. *Redeemed us* (**v. 7**)—bought us back from sin, Satan, and damnation.

e. *Forgives us* (**v. 7**)—gives us the blessings of His redemption.

f. *Makes His mysteries known to us* (**v.9**). This is the whole process of God revealing Himself to us through the means of grace. It is the one activity that God allows the church to partake in.

g. *Brings all things together in Christ* (**v. 10**)—the final act in which God will gather the chosen for the final time to be with Him forever.

God does these actions: (a) always; (b) from eternity; (c) from eternity; (d) when Christ died; (e) every day; (f) when His Word is taught; (g) on Judgment Day.

Verses 15-22

1. To demonstrate God's activity for His chosen, Paul enumerates what he himself remembers to include in his prayers on behalf of the Ephesians: for the Spirit; to give wisdom and revelation; for enlightenment to know of their inheritance and of their hope in Christ.

2. The mighty acts of God as seen in the life of Christ are: raised from the dead; seated in heaven in all power forever; rules all things for the benefit of His church.

3. In **verse 23** Paul uses the term *His body* as a description of the church. See **1 Cor. 12** for more information on this analogy.

4. Use this question to reinforce the connection between the opening story and being a "called-out one." Ask, **What have you been called out to do?**

PRACTICE (Objectives 1 and 4)

1. Define the terms together in class. Some students may never have heard the words. For others this will be a review. Help students understand the meanings for their lives.

Grace—God's undeserved kindness
Paul—apostle to the Gentiles, author of Ephesians
saints—the faithful in Christ Jesus
Ephesus—a large seaport in Asia Minor, location of a congregation composed of both Jewish and Gentile Christians
Jesus—Savior
Lord—true God, Creator, Ruler
Christ—the Anointed One, Messiah
predestined—chosen by God for an eteranal destiny of salvation
church—ecclesia, "called-out ones," the body of Christ

2. Assign this as a take-home activity. To keep from embarrassing students who have not always been Lutherans, encourage them to substitute other events of spiritual importance. This activity will provide an opportunity for you to discuss the importance of baptism with them.

3. Following are suggested answers: a, d, f, g, h, and j—congregation; b and c—called-out ones; e and i—both.

We did not introduce the terms "visible" and "invisible" church. If you feel they would help your students better understand the concept, you might discuss how they relate to "community of called-out ones" and "congregation."

4. Divide the class into groups of three or four. Ask them to talk about answers for the Student Book questions. Then discuss their responses with the entire class. Be sure they describe their importance in God's church family and that they recognize that only through God's grace do we become part of His body, the church. He empowers us to live as His "called-out ones."

MEMORY

Each Student Book session will ordinarily contain at least one Bible verse. You might use these representative verses as the basis for a memorization course. Otherwise use them to help your students summarize a main point from the lesson.

WRAP-UP

Assign **"Practice"** 2 for use in the next session. You might then tell the class what you know of your baptism and confirmation. Finish with your personal prayer of thanks to God for including you in His church.

Session 2: God Makes It Work

BIBLE BASIS: Col. 1:1–14

CENTRAL TRUTH

God called us through the Gospel and made us members of the church. He also empowers us to demonstrate that membership in our lives.

OBJECTIVES

That the students will
1. name individuals who had a part in bringing the Gospel to them;
2. describe the process of the Gospel being transmitted throughout the world;
3. pray for fellow Christians;
4. identify the signs of faith within the church as seen in the fruits of the Spirit;
5. express gratefulness for being included in the church, having been rescued by Christ from the power of

BACKGROUND

"Why am I a Christian?"

You've probably asked yourself this question dozens of times. And you've probably answered each time that you didn't make yourself a Christian. You know that would have been impossible. You know that God is the One who acted for you. He sent His Son to earn your salvation. He led individuals to share the Gospel with you, perhaps when you were an infant. He provides for you through the church, again and again strengthening your faith, lifting you up from moments of doubt or depression.

One of your primary challenges as a teacher of religion in a Lutheran high school is to provide information, settings, and a personal witness so your students come to the same kinds of realizations. Of course, it's God who is acting through you, and He will also bless your work. In today's session, students will have an opportunity to examine their spiritual roots and to share some of the blessings God gives them and others through the church.

STRETCHING (Objective 1)

Use the questionnaire from session 1 to regenerate interest in how the class members came into the church. As you discuss:

1. Be positive in all your comments on contributions.

2. Try to draw out everyone—but also recognize that some students prefer to absorb and not comment.

3. Use humor whenever possible to create a relaxed climate.

When the activity has fulfilled its usefulness, go on to the Bible study.

GETTING THE WORD (Objectives 2-4)

Some background material is presented in the Student Book. You might wish to add some information on the city of Colossae from Bible dictionaries, commentaries, or handbooks.

Verses 1-2

Much of these two greetings is similar: the order; Paul's identification of himself; the term "faithful"; the use of "grace and peace."

Differences include: "Timothy our brother"; the substitution of "brothers" for "saints"; the elimination of "and the Lord Jesus Christ."

Verses 3-8

This section provides a fairly clear outline of how the Gospel is transmitted to the world. The Gospel was transmitted through people and brought fruit as it spread through the world.

1. Paul refers to "the Gospel that has come to you." (vv. 5-6).

2. Epaphras brought the Gospel to the Colossians.

3. The Gospel was "bearing fruit and growing" (v. 6). That's the promise God still makes to His congregations today!

You might want to put the diagram on the board and fill in the names of

apostles and helpers and the congregations they started or worked in (e.g., Paul—Corinth; John—Ephesus; Luke—Philippi)

Verse 9

In working through this verse, remind the students that spiritual leaders also have the responsibility of accounting for their flock (Heb. 13:17). As time allows, read and discuss John 17:6-26 and Phil. 1:3-11. Emphasize that those who bring the Gospel need to be in close communication with "headquarters" to know how to do the work.

Verses 10-12

1. Paul indicates that the motivation for a Christian life is that we "may please Him" (v. 10). Our Christian life is a way of thanking the Lord for our salvation, not of earning it.

2. The words and phrases that show Christian witness are live a life worthy of the Lord; please Him; "bearing fruit;" "growing;" "being strengthened;" "may have great endurance and patience;" "giving thanks;" "to share." All of these are signs of the Spirit at work in the church.

Verses 13-14

This is a beautiful summary of the Gospel, worthy of memorizing.

PRACTICE (Objectives 3-5)

1. Do this activity as a class project, using transparencies and an overhead projector or a large chalkboard. Use one or two student resumes. Fill in the path of the Gospel from the first century to the time when some students can name ancestors. Don't overlook how the Gospel came to minority people. To fill in this information, consult an encyclopedia, the *Lutheran Cyclopedia* (Concordia, 1975), a church-history text, a world-history text, or a veteran pastor.

2. Carefully read through Gal. 5:22-23 with the class and explain what each fruit might look like. As you do this, have them jot down names.

This activity can be mutually

uplifting if the students genuinely recognize these traits in each other or in the faculty. As always, keep this positive as names are suggested.

3. If your class is spiritually mature enough to handle this, great benefits can occur (especially one week from now when they get together to discuss how the various prayers were answered).

If you feel your class is not ready for this kind of assignment, have each individual write his or her own needs on the paper, fold it with the name on outside, and deposit it in a "vault" for one week. Tell them to put these needs into their prayers for this week.

At the end of that time, redistribute the papers and allow each student privately to consider how God answered those prayers.

4. Do not pressure students to share these reflections. If some wish to, consider it a plus.

Regard each student's book as his or her own private collection of spiritual produce. Many may wish to look back on their thoughts later on in life.

WRAP-UP
Close with your own prayer, thanking the Lord for rescuing us from the power of sin and Satan. Or ask a student volunteer to pray.

Session 3: God's Miracle

BIBLE BASIS: Eph. 2:1-18

CENTRAL TRUTH
God builds His church by raising to spiritual life all whom He has chosen. Whether Jew or Gentile, He saves all in the same way, by grace through faith in Jesus Christ.

OBJECTIVES
That the students will
1. identify the marks of spiritual death;
2. describe how completely powerless we are to save ourselves;
3. explain that conversion is entirely an act of a loving and gracious God;
4. explain that all people and all races are saved in the same way;
5. describe the conflict between spiritual life and death and the struggle Christians still face in this conflict.

BACKGROUND
The world today beckons us to "be all you can be." That sounds OK, and in the best sense it is. God gives us talents and wants us to develop them to His glory. Too often, though, we emphasize "you can be" as if no one else--especially not God--has anything to do with our destiny.

That's the mind-set your students face day by day. "Lift yourself up by your bootstraps." "Make something of yourself." It feels good when we feel responsibility for a success, and society urges us to grab hold of the credit for every good thing that happens to us. But salvation just does not work that way. *God* chose us. *God* redeemed us. *God* made us His sons and daughters. And *God* empowers us to demonstrate His love to others. That's the miracle you will talk about in this session. Pray that God will bless your teaching and bring increased faith and joy to your students!

Getting Ready.
Be sure to find newspapers and magazines for Practice, 1.

STRETCHING
The introductory story is self-explanatory and should lead without comment into the Bible study. More time than usual is to be spent on this portion of Ephesians since it presents one of the main tenets of our faith--salvation by grace through faith. Therefore allow enough time to discuss this reading thoroughly.

GETTING THE WORD (Objectives 1-4)

Verses 1-3
These verses deal with our natural condition. All humanity faces the predicament of being "dead in . . .

trangressions and sins" (v. 1). Paul goes into this subject more thoroughly in Rom. 1—2. Student material in this session does not try to personify and describe Satan, "the ruler of the kingdom of the air" (v. 2), since he will be discussed in more detail in unit 8. Also, emphasize the universal mess humanity is in, not how it got there.

1. The following can be sources of the "odor of spiritual death": Mass disobedience, corporate and petty theft, drug and alcohol abuse, the selfish use of sex, the media's appeal to greed, the emphasis on the occult, etc.

2. In v. 3, we probably refers to Jews, and the rest to Gentiles; all of us (Jews and Gentiles) are by nature spiritually dead.

3. The end of being spiritually dead comes at the time of baptism for infants. For others that happens at the time faith comes alive within them.

Verses 4—10

Emphasize all the action initiated and carried out by God: "His great love . . . made us alive . . . God raised us up, seated us with Him . . . [to] show . . . riches of His grace, expressed in His kindness . . . by grace you have been saved . . . gift of God . . . God prepared in advance." Students should recognize that our part in this is nil.

In 2:4, 6 and 10 Paul mentions the miracles of (1) "raising from the dead" and (2) creating. This terminology is no accident. It shows that we do not "make a decision," "decide," or "choose to follow." This terminology is quite popular today among nondenomination-alists. It implies that we have a part in our conversion. These passages blow that theory apart.

Verses 11—18

The tension in Ephesus may have been caused by the age-old conflict between Jew and Gentile. For more on this read Acts 15:1—19 and Gal. 2:11—21. Be sure that students recognize that both Jew and Gentile are saved "through the blood of Christ" (v. 13).

People sometimes ask how people in the Old Testament were saved, inasmuch as Christ had not come yet. The answer is the same: saved by grace through faith in the Savior yet to come.

"You who were far away" (v.17) refers to the Gentiles and those who were near refers to the Jews.

Point 4 in the Student Book is crucial. Probably the moment of conversion for many of your students came at their baptism. Since they cannot remember this, put them at ease by point out that salvation is not dependent on our remembering or feeling anything. It is solely based on God's grace.

PRACTICE (Objectives 1—3 and 5)

1. Prepare for this by bringing to class an adequate number of newspapers and magazines. You can also screen content. Keep the groups small enough so they will stay on the subject. Do not be alarmed if individuals obviously enjoy looking for "trash." Try to get representative examples from all areas of life.

2. Use the same procedure as in 1. If necessary, review Gal. 5:22—23 or Session 2 so everyone understands "Fruits of the Spirit." Don't be surprised if groups don't find much. The media, like flies, thrive on filth.

3. Use this activity to tie 1 and 2 together. Carefully read and interpret Paul's conflict in Rom. 7:14—25. Vent your own frustrations with this conflict. Point out that this warfare shows that spiritual life exists (otherwise one never senses a conflict). Also point out that a Christian looks back with disgust on those times when the sinful nature wins. Here is where forgiveness comes in.

4. The situations that are suggested for completion are: Jesus would . . .
a. Look for a job at . . .
b. Go out for . . .
c. Go to a party at . . .
d. Subscribe to . . .
e. Listen to . . .
f. Turn on a TV set and watch . . .
g. Be good friends with . . .
h. Plan to become . . .
i. Prefer to eat at . . .
j. Like to talk about . . .
This activity could lead to some

deep insights into student perceptions of Christ. Allow student to have fun but not to become disrespectful. Through this activity students may become more aware that Jesus is a real person, living alongside them.

WRAP-UP
Conclude with a time for silent meditation or rereading of **Eph. 2:1-18.** Encourage sentence prayers from volunteers.

Session 4: God's Building Project

BIBLE BASIS: Eph. 2:19-22

CENTRAL TRUTH
An ancient temple provides a picture of God's church, built to the glory of God by the Spirit; unified by and dependent upon Christ, the cornerstone; composed of believers of all races and of all time.

OBJECTIVES
That the students will
1. analyze and explain the analogy of a temple being a picture of the church;
2. explain how Jesus Christ is the perfect unifier of the Old and New Testaments, of Jews and Gentiles;
3. describe their status and possible place in God's church;
4. suggest ways to apply this analogy to their lives.

BACKGROUND
These few verses are filled with terms that will need explanation for students to understand the message (e.g., foreigners, aliens, fellow citizens, foundation, cornerstone, temple). Use as much time as necessary to provide this background.

Pray that God will use you as His instrument to open the door to new insights for members of your class. What does it mean to them, for example, to be a "brick" in the same building that contains Christ as the cornerstone, the apostles and prophets as the foundation, and people like Martin Luther as other "bricks"?

STRETCHING (Objective 1)
Use more time than usual on this section, since it will provide background information to help students understand the analogy that follows. Following are some points to stress.
1. The temple of Artemis (Diana)

was a mecca for immoral worship. Session 24 comes back to it. Paul used the idea of a temple only to illustrate a much more important concept, the church. He certainly was not condoning the activities that went on there!
2. Use the Student Book illustration to clarify the various parts of the temple and to show how its integrity depended on the cornerstone.
3. Apparently the ancients were able to move such huge stones by using massed human (slave) power, sleds, rollers, inclined planes, and tremendous organization.
4. As a further mind-boggler, mention to the students that Solomon's temple was built of stones quarried over 100 miles away, cut to the exact size, brought to the site and put into place without the sound of hammer or chisel **(1 Kings 6:7).** (See also **1 Kings 7:1-12** for a description of Solomon's palace.) Note that it took only 7 years to complete the temple **(1 Kings 6:38)**!
5. Point out the variety of materials that were used for various purposes in such a temple. Even today we are often astonished by the variety of materials that go into a building. The analogy makes the point that God can use the talents of people in some way. You will return to this in session 5.

GETTING THE WORD (Objectives 1--2)
As a change of pace, have the students read and work out this part on their own. Be available to explain words or concepts but do not supply answers.

You and your students may have two different agendas as they complete this activity. You will want them to gain experiences in self-Bible study and to use appropriate thought processes as they work. Their agenda may say, "Get all the answers correct" and "Get done." If so, they will probably try to get the answers from you or some other source instead of thinking through the questions. Use firm but friendly procedures to steer them into doing some real thinking.

After students complete the activity, consider having them check their own work, adding information they may have missed. A score or grade from you seems minor compared to learning and believing the concepts.

1. The Gentiles "are no longer foreigners and aliens" (v. 19).

2. The Jews are "God's people and members of God's household" (v. 19).

3. In Christ, Gentiles and Jews have equal status as members of God's family.

4. The foundation stones are the apostles and prophets (v. 20).

5. Following are some possible similarities between God's Word and foundation stones:
--The Old and New Testaments were written (put in place) by God's "superhuman" effort.
--Each book has strength and perfection, qualities needed in a foundation stone.
--In spite of varying form and authorship, the books of the Bible fit together perfectly.
--The Bible does not need outside reinforcement.

6. Following are some possible similarities between Jesus Christ and the cornerstone:
--Christ is the most important, unifying message of the Old and New Testaments.
--All teachings in the Bible begin and end in Christ.
--Jesus is also perfect, everlasting, unchangeable, the perfect Truth.
--Jesus ties the Old and New Testaments together.
--Our entire faith rests in the Lord of the Scriptures, not on the people or events recorded in it.

7. The church is built on Christ alone. The things we believe and practice are based solely on what He did for us. He saves everyone in the same way. Therefore there is no difference of status or value. All members of the church contribute their lives and talents to the glory of God.

8. Since God lives in and through each believer, the gathering of believers truly becomes the dwelling place of God.

9. God expects us to be a priesthood, giving to God the sacrifices of our lives as a thanksgiving for what Jesus did for us.

10. 1 Peter 2:9-10 is similar to Eph. 2:14-18.

11. (Ps. 118:22 is the source for the quotation in 1 Peter 2:7b.) The Jewish religious leaders (scribes, Pharisees, priests) rejected Jesus as the Messiah (the capstone).

PRACTICE (Objective 3)
Handle this activity very carefully. Students are asked to provide very personal information, possibly about ideas they have never thought about before. Help them understand their role in the analogy of being "stones" ready to be fit into the church.

No "right" or "wrong" answers are intended. Honor responses as very personal. Students in a mature class might talk together about how each perceives himself or herself. In a less mature group, students might confide their opinions with a close friend. Or, if both the above seem too threatening, just encourage a simple "do it by yourself" and "check back later to see if anything has changed."

WRAP-UP (Objective 4)
The closing activity provides an opportunity for "the living stones" to do something together. Welcome personal comments on images they have about their part of the house of the Lord.

Session 5: God's Collection of Gifts

BIBLE BASIS: 1 Cor. 12:1-31

CENTRAL TRUTH

God places people with many different gifts into His church. The Holy Spirit uses them all to accomplish His purposes. These members are all unified in Christ.

OBJECTIVES

That the students will

1. identify the Holy Spirit as the One who gives to the church the gifts it needs;

2. state that spiritual gifts come only to those who, because the Holy Spirit empowers them, confess that Jesus Christ is Lord;

3. enumerate the gifts from the Holy Spirit and the value of each;

4. describe the problems of diversity and how Christ can bring order and purpose to such diversity.

BACKGROUND

"No one can say, 'Jesus is Lord,' except by the Holy Spirit" (1 Cor. 12:3).

No teacher can lead students to believe in and to follow their Savior except by the Holy Spirit.

Some discussions of spiritual gifts generate more heat than light. Pray that God will empower you to present His message clearly. Make your message the same as Paul's: We receive spiritual gifts for the common good.

STRETCHING (Objective 1)

Do not spend much time on this introduction. Use it simply to present the concept of the Holy Spirit giving gifts to the church. If necessary, quickly review the doctrine of the Holy Spirit with the students who are not familiar with Him.

GETTING THE WORD (Objectives 1—4)

Most of the discussion centers on 1 Cor. 12 instead of Eph. 4 because of its emphasis on naming the gifts of the Spirit and those who produce them. 1 Cor. 12 also includes the analogy of the human body to the church.

1 Cor. 12:1-3

We apprehend God's gifts through faith in Jesus, and this occurs only by the power of the Holy Spirit. No one dare make the claim that we, even in some small way, "decided" to become a child of God.

1 Cor. 12:4-11

1. God gives spiritual gifts for **the common good (v. 7).** In Eph. 4:12 Paul adds, **to prepare God's people for works of service, so that the body of Christ may be built up.**

2. Work together on the list in 1 Cor. 12:8-10, using the board or overhead projector. The "Now" portion of the list will vary according to current "gifts" to the church. Most Bible scholars agree that "faith" (v. 9) refers to the heroic faith that can "move mountains" **(Matt. 17:20).** The apostles used this faith, for example, in connection with gifts of healing and miraculous powers. It seems that God gives spiritual gifts as they are needed in the church, and that few, if any, Christians today have gifts such as healing, miraculous powers, ability to speak in tongues, and interpretation of tongues. As you discuss these gifts, emphasize again and again that God gives them for the common good, and not to create divisions within His church.

For the "Then" portion, students might think of Paul himself, Peter, John, Stephen, Luke, Jude, and others.

3. One benefit of spiritual gifts used for the common good is that the church grows and pospers (Eph. 4:15-16).

1 Cor. 12:12-27

You might have students try to find out how many times Paul repeats (in different words) the message of verse 12 (**"though all its parts are many, they form one body"**). Compare this with his emphasis **"for the common good"** (v. 7). Contemporary messages should emphasize how we use our gifts for the benefit of others in God's church.

1 Cor. 12:28–31

1 and 2. Students should discover that Paul mentions some gifts twice (e.g., prophets, workers of miracles, those with gifts of healing, those speaking in tongues), while he names some only in the first list (e.g., message of knowledge, faith) or the second list (e.g., apostles, those able to help others, those with gifts of administration). These differences, combined with differences in lists in **Rom. 12** and **Eph. 4,** suggest that God does not necessarily provide the same gifts to all people in His church at all times. Rather, He gives His people whatever gifts His church needs to accomplish His purposes at a given time.

3. Note the context of these verses. Just before this, Paul emphasized that each part of the body (the church) is important as it contributes to the whole ("for the common good"—v. 7). Then, in **1 Cor. 13,** he writes about love, the characteristic that *must* exist when we use our gifts.

As necessary, spend some time with the gifts of speaking in tongues and interpreting tongues, especially since Paul wrote in **1 Cor. 14** about problems in the Corinthian church related to those gifts. God may not give this gift to His church today. If He does, He certainly wants us to follow the guidelines of **1 Cor. 13—14** to use this gift with a spirit of love and humility instead of a spirit of pride.

Eph. 4:14–16

1. In this discourse on spiritual gifts, Paul says that acting like an infant (that is, having no solid position; doing what is expedient, going with the flow) is a sign of the body of Christ out of control. This happens in the body and in the church, when there is no control or communication from the Head.

2. Confusion in the church can be eliminated through direct control by Christ.

3. Confusion in the church ends when we follow Christ's love, His life, His way. When all members operate only out of love to Christ and to each other, pride, envy, and strife will end. We give Christ control when we find out what He has said and done, and then do things His way.

PRACTICE (Objective 4)

1 and 2. As you roleplay, be sure to emphasize the message, not the method. Many 10th-graders enjoy roleplaying, but the following suggestions may help you achieve success:
 --Don't force anyone to act. Some people just don't want to.
 --A set of phones or a microphone makes a good prop. These tools seem natural for teenagers. They also provide something for their hands to do.
 --Stop the episode when repetition sets in.
 --Enjoy the acting. Laughter encourages more freedom of expression.
 --Sum up each episode by referring to points from the lesson, pluses or minuses related to the acting.
 Use both sets of situations to dramatize the foolishness of petty pride and envy.

3. Involve everyone in this writing activity. You may want each student to write on more than one topic. You could use the last one (d) as a class discussion catalyst.

Unit 2: How the Church Lives

Since the church is God's creation, it, like all of God's creatures, shows signs of life. These signs of life are the subject of this unit.

Your class will discover that God's method of sustaining life in the church comes through the ministry of each member to the other. Such ministry involves hearing God's Word and receiving the sacraments--in other words, *the means of grace.* Another evidence of life in the church is its willingness to bear witness to the world of its faith in Christ.

The church is not an organization that is in existence just to exist.

No, the church exists to give away the grace it has received from a loving God.

The unit concludes with a review of units 1 and 2.

Session 6: Sticking Together

BIBLE BASIS: Rom. 1:8–17

CENTRAL TRUTH

God uses the members of the church to strengthen and encourage one another personally through the Gospel.

OBJECTIVES

That the students will

1. describe the power of the Gospel in converting sinners and in sustaining faith;

2. identify situations where Christians can share the Gospel with fellow Christians;

3. show evidence of the joy they experience from giving good news to each other;

4. express appreciation of the community of believers who minister to each other.

BACKGROUND

At the beginning of this new unit, **"Stretching"** presents a short review. It ties together some of Paul's analogies from the last unit with the concept of Christians helping each other with their faith.

Before you teach, decide whether you will write the phrases on the board, on chart paper, or on a transparency. Consider preparing these phrases before class.

Also decide in advance how you will organize your class for **"Practice."** The activity will probably work best if members of each group know each other well enough to be able to pick out some good traits of all members of the group, though the group conversations may provide enough information for them to complete the activity successfully.

Pray that God will not only lead your class to understand how members of the body of Christ can and should work together, but that He will also create caring relationships within your classroom (your special unit within the body of Christ).

STRETCHING (Objective 2)

Have the students write their answers in the book and then check them as you read the correct responses. Following is the list of correct responses in the correct order. You, of course, need to mix them up when writing them on the board, chart, or transparency.

1. The Holy Spirit = a deposit on a guarantee

2. Good works = fruit

3. Satan's kingdom = the dominion of darkness

4. Our former life under Satan = dead spiritually

5. The Law with commandments and regulations = wall of hostility

6. The Old and New Testaments = foundations of a temple

7. Jesus Christ = chief cornerstone of a temple

8. Believers = living stones in a temple

9. The church = a body

10. Those who work in the church = gifts

Use this only as an introduction, being sure to make the transition as described in the Student Book. Besides being an eminent scholar, Paul was an excellent teacher, making frequent use of analogies and comparisons. Paul used these to help his readers grow spiritually--always the goal of his epistles.

GETTING THE WORD (Objectives 1--2 and 4)

Verses 8–10

As you talk about the relationship between Paul and the Roman Christians, think about the relationship you have with your students. Imagine how you would feel if parents, fellow teachers, and other students would speak in glowing terms about the faith of those in your class! Tell your students how this would make you feel.

Verses 11-13

These verses contain the key to this lesson. Paul wanted to come personally to visit them so that both he and they could build up each other's faith (v. 12). Paul would build them up by giving to them *wisdom, knowledge, faith*, etc., as listed in 1 Cor. 12:7-10. When Paul actually did arrive in Rome as a prisoner, and after having little success with the Jews, he spent his time, in his own house, preaching and teaching about the Lord Jesus Christ (Acts 28:31). Note in Acts 28:15 that Paul "thanked God and was encouraged" by the sight of these Roman Christians.

We often receive spiritual encouragement from our pastors and teachers. This we expect. So we tend to feel more excitement when personal encouragement comes from friends, relatives, and associates--from less likely sources (at least so it seems to us). Encourage the students to name those who have helped them spiritually. Delve beyond the obvious.

In **verse 12** Paul states that he also would benefit from the faith of the Romans. In working through the various settings presented, consider this the heart of the lesson. Encourage the students to think of examples outside of church. The church extends into homes, schools, teams, and places of work.

When Paul speaks of a harvest (v. 13), he is referring to the same harvest of souls that Jesus spoke of in **Matt. 9:37**.

Verses 14-15

From **v. 16** and from the list of people Paul greets in **chapter 16**, we can deduce that the Jews and Gentiles were represented in the Roman congregation quite evenly. As we read in **Eph. 2:19-22**, all are made one in Christ and therefore can live together in the unity of His Spirit.

Verses 16-17

The Student Book refers to the power and importance of this passage. In 1 Cor. 1:23 Paul calls the preaching of the cross "foolishness." To the logical mind of a Roman, a Jew executed on a cross as payment for all of humanity's errors indeed would sound stupid. But Paul was not ashamed to proclaim this loud and clear, even in the face of ridicule.

The Greek word for "power" is "dynamis," our root for *dynamite*. Conversion through the Gospel message demonstrates the life-giving explosion of faith. Further irony of the Gospel is that God's absolute holiness (righteousness) is applied to the sinner through faith. Indeed, the newly righteous, the believer, lives eternally by faith and not by works. Paul says more about this miracle in **Rom. 3:22**.

Finally, we have the great joy and privilege to tell the Good News to each other in a personal way. In so doing, we are building up each other's faith and joy in the Lord.

PRACTICE (Objectives 3--4)

See "**Background**" for suggestions for dividing the class into groups. Then follow the Student Book procedures. While the students will not necessarily tell the Gospel to each other, yet they will give each other "good news." The results should be obvious as the activity ends.

WRAP-UP

If you have a mature class, you could have the small groups stay together and quietly pray for each other, thanking the Lord for each other.

Session 7: Listening Together

BIBLE BASIS: 1 Tim. 4

CENTRAL TRUTH

God uses His Word to build up His church. As members receive this Word through reading, preaching, and teaching, He strengthens their faith.

OBJECTIVES

That the student will
1. Identify false teachings and problems that arise in the church when

we fail to use God's Word;

    2. describe the importance of hearing and reading God's Word; personally and in their congregations

    3. recall their past exposure to God's Word;

    4. list the local congregation's use of the Bible;

    5. share their experiences in praying for and with each other.

BACKGROUND

In **1 Timothy** we read encouragement and advice from an experienced pastor to a young pastor. Timothy was a young convert from Lystra whom Paul met during his first missionary journey. Under his instruction Timothy became a trusted loyal coworker.

Apparently Paul wrote **1 Timothy** while Timothy was at Ephesus, trying to lead this rather large mixture of believers. In **1 Tim. 4**, Paul was warning Timothy of the dangers of false doctrine, a product of Satan himself. Paul pointed Timothy toward the Word of God in strong doses, lovingly administered by teaching and preaching.

STRETCHING

Use this activity to lead into the lesson. Here are the answers (with references for further examination).

    1. A boy listening to Jesus preach; **John 6:8**
    2. David; **1 Sam. 21:1–6**
    3. Samson; **Judg. 14:8–9**
    4. Daniel and friends; **Dan. 1:8–14**
    5. Elijah; **1 Kings 19:5–6**
    6. God and two angels; **Gen. 18:1–8**
    7. Children of Israel; **Ex. 16:31**
    8. Ezekiel, John; **Ezek. 3:1–2; Rev. 10:8–10**
    9. Esau; **Gen. 25:29–34**

Make the transition to the lesson as indicated. The analogy of the body of Christ is used with the idea that a body has to eat, and the food for this body is the Word of God. Do not make the distinction yet between the Bible and the sacraments. The sacraments are based on the Word of God with the added dimension of visible means. This concept will be developed in the next session.

GETTING THE WORD (Objectives 1–2)

First read the entire chapter. Then discuss it section by section. Use the questions mainly as starters. During the discussion encourage questions and comments from the students.

Verses 1–4

1. To many people, junk food tastes good, but it provides little nutrition. A diet of too much junk food can lead to malnutrition.

2. Abstaining from marriage and prohibiting certain foods sounds like the work of Judaizers. This group wished to retain Old Testament laws. Today false teachings include those related to the End Time (millennialism, rapture); conversion (humans assist in God's work); the person of Christ (not true God); and Satan (he doesn't exist). Spend some time extracting others.

Verses 6–8

1. In **Mark 7:18–19**, Jesus plainly did away with all prohibitions against certain foods. Knowing what Jesus said should end any controversy on that subject.

2. The church needs to be sure of what Christ has said in the Gospels and through the entire New Testament. Satan indeed attacks where he detects that we are not sure of God's instructions.

Verses 9–11

1. Our faith rests on what these words say. Christ is our only hope of salvation. All other doctrines are based on this truth. The church's witness can be gauged on how clearly it enunciates this truth.

2. Our command, as in **Matt. 28**, is to teach this to all nations as effectively as possible.

Verses 12–16

1. Paul told Timothy to preach and teach God's Word publicly "until I come." God gives us the same command: "Do this until I come at the end of time."

2. The church's preaching and teaching ministries fulfill this. Think also of ministries to those who are sick or have disabilities such as mental retardation and blindness.

3. Publicly these ministries are

done through the organized church. Privately, they are done by individuals who day by day tell and live the Gospel to their acquaintances.

4. As we grow in the Word, God empowers our will to follow His will, causes our prayer to become more meaningful, and makes Scripture easier to understand.

5. God moves a congregation to exhibit these same skills: Love for Bible study, outreach to the needy, rejection of false doctrine, mission-mindedness, etc.

6. Let the maturity of your class determine how much you will discuss this question.

PRACTICE (Objectives 3--5)

1. Allow this to be a private activity. If some wish, let students share experiences.

2. Your board may not be large enough to contain the means of communication available.

3. Besides those given: sermon; various readings; choir music; liturgical parts such as psalm readings; creeds; sacraments. All these proclaim the Word.

4. This follow-up to session 2 can be done at some other time, but is a natural here, since it is so closely related to God's Word among us.

WRAP-UP

Consider ending with prayers for each other in the above groups. If group work cannot be done, have a good reader reread **1 Tim. 4:1-15** as a meditation.

Session 8: Receiving Together

BIBLE BASIS: Matt. 28:16-20; 1 Cor. 11:23-26

CENTRAL TRUTH

In the two sacraments, Holy Baptism and Holy Communion, God uses His Word and physical means to convey to us His love in Christ.

OBJECTIVES

That the students will

1. explain how God gives His grace to us in the sacraments of Baptism and the Lord's Supper;

2. describe appropriate uses of both sacraments;

3. receive answers to their questions about the Sacraments;

4. describe acceptable variations in usage (without changing the meanings) of the sacraments.

BACKGROUND

The format of this session has been designed to help you achieve objectives 1 and 3. If your students come from a variety of backgrounds, they will not all understand the sacraments the same way. Therefore the first part of the session is devoted to reteaching the doctrines of the sacraments. Use the last part of the session to answer questions raised in the students' minds during the first part.

This session probably contains more material than you can use in one period. You will need to choose the activities that best fill the needs of your class.

As you prepare for this session, review how other denominations view the sacraments, especially the denominations of students in your class.

Pray that the Holy Spirit will move all your students to believe what He tells us about the sacraments in Scripture.

STRETCHING

This fictional story refers to a document issued by some southern states before the Civil War. It could be offered as proof that the individual was indeed a free man or woman. After the Emancipation Proclamation, no such documents were issued.

GETTING THE WORD (Objectives 1--2)

Understanding Baptism and Holy Communion

The "Stretching" story is an analogy illustrating the two sacraments of the church. Following are some of the different teachings about the sacraments among various Christian denominations.

Roman Catholics teach that God gave 7 sacraments. They baptize all, including infants, using water and the Word, usually applied by sprinkling. They teach that in Communion the bread and wine are changed into Christ's body and blood (transubstantiation). First Communion: children at age 6 or 7.

Lutherans teach that God gave 2 sacraments. We baptize all, including infants, using water and the Word, usually applied by washing, pouring, or sprinkling. We teach that in Communion God gives His body and blood in, with, and under the bread and wine (Real Presence). First Communion: teenagers and adults after instruction.

Most *Protestant Reformed* denominations teach that God gave 2 sacraments (sometimes called rites or ordinances). Many of them baptize only after a believer can verbalize his or her faith, and prefer to baptize by immersion (though this practice varies). They teach that in Communion the bread and wine represent Christ's body and blood. Age of first Communion varies.

Take time to explain the Lutheran doctrines of both Baptism and Holy Communion. Stress that both are means (pathways) through which God gives His grace to us.

The chart can be filled out this way:

Topic	The Story	The Church
1. The gifts	Letter, document, carving	God's Word, Baptism, Communion
2. The giver	Grandfather	God
3. The reason	Love	Love
4. The receiver	James	The church
5. Object that explains	Letter	The Bible
6. Object that frees	Document	Baptism
7. Object that remembers	Carving of stallion	Holy Communion
8. Person who transmits gifts	Mother	Church
9. Feelings generated	Love, joy, confidence	Love, joy, confidence

Don't try to fit every detail of the story into the analogical meaning. For instance, the fact that the carving was a stallion has no special significance. Spend discussion time on the main **points**.

Some Questions About Baptism and Holy Communion

If you have copies of the Catechism available, use them to get more detail into Luther's teachings. Answer the questions together as a class activity.

1. Baptism offers the forgiveness of sins and assurance of salvation. Each day we recall our baptism, God gives us new power to "drown the old man." We receive a new start for a new day.

2. A person can lose faith through neglect and indifference. Faith in God's salvation saves us. When the faith generated in baptism dies, so does salvation.

3. Infants are also a part of "all nations." Infants, too, can believe, even though they cannot verbalize their faith. Infant baptism testifies to the fact that conversion is entirely God's miracle.

4. Jesus clearly states: **"This is My body. This is My blood."** We have no reason to say that Jesus meant "represents." Also in **1 Cor. 11:27**, Paul clearly says that an unworthy reception results in sinning against the **body and blood** of the Lord.

5. The words, **whenever you eat this bread and drink this cup (1 Cor. 11:26)** suggest that we should partake of the Lord's Supper regularly. The early church communed at least once each week.

6. The words of Jesus and Paul encourage us to commune whenever we feel a need for forgiveness and reassurance. A proper celebration does not depend on an emotional high, but on Christ's presence.

PRACTICE (Objectives 3—4)

1. Students should have raised many

questions by this time. If not, use this activity to encourage questions. Insure anonymity and enforce a climate of nonridicule. Answer whatever questions you can. If you don't know the answers, be honest and tell them so. But do try to find the answers to share on another day.

2. Use this alternative if your students do not have questions, but have strong congregational ties.

Variations in practice will surface. Respect honest variation, but correct faulty doctrine.

WRAP-UP
Conclude by offering a prayer of thanks for both sacraments. Use a prayer from the Lutheran Agenda for after a baptism or use a post-Communion prayer.

Session 9: Working Together

BIBLE BASIS: Titus 2

CENTRAL TRUTH
Having received God's grace through Word and Sacrament, the church now becomes Christ's witness to the world. In every age and in every occupation, God uses it to continue Christ's work of reconciling the world to Himself.

OBJECTIVES
That the students will

1. demonstrate that they recall the major emphases of sessions 1 to 8;

2. retrace the steps Christ took in redeeming humanity, including the activities of His ministry that led to His death and resurrection;

3. describe how they can be Christ's representatives to the world;

4. identify ways they can witness to their Lord at every age and in every occupation.

BACKGROUND
In session 8 you reviewed (or taught) the blessings we receive from God through the sacraments. By now everyone should be developing a clear concept of how God creates and strengthens faith through Word and Sacrament.

In this session you will look at our response to the blessings we receive from God's grace. Paul's letter to Titus places this response into the context of encouraging others by sound doctrine and refuting those who oppose it (Titus 1:9). In chapter 2 Paul gives advice to various groups within the church: older men, older women, younger women, young men, and slaves. Students will also examine advice from

other parts of Paul's epistles that apply to these groups--and to similar groups today.

Pray that the Holy Spirit will move your students to believe God's Word and "to say 'No' to ungodliness and worldy passions, and to live self-controlled, upright and godly lives in this present age" (Titus 2:12).

STRETCHING (Objective 1)
The introductory activity reviews concepts from sessions 1 to 8. It anticipates session 10, which is a review of units 1 and 2.

As necessary, help students focus on the major points you have discussed.

1. God created the church ("called-out ones," ecclesia).

2. God makes it work by means of the Gospel (the Good News; those who tell it in word and deed).

3. God's miracle is conversion (raising us to spiritual life).

4. God's building project is the church (each member, a part; Christ, the Cornerstone).

5. God's collection of gifts are individual church members (each contributes talents to the work).

6. The church sticks together when its members encourage each other's faith.

7. The church listens together to God's Word (God's method of sustaining and building faith).

8. The church receives God's grace through His Word, Baptism, and Holy Communion.

GETTING THE WORD (Objectives 2--3)
This session will help recall exactly what it was that Christ did for

us. Read each reference together. Fill in gaps of background, but do not dwell on each individual story.

1. Jesus came to give His life so that all who believe in Him will have everlasting life.

2. Jesus demonstrated God's love by healing, raising the dead, and preaching the Good News.

3. The reference is Is. 61:1–2. (If necessary, show students how to use cross-references or footnotes to find this answer.)

4. Point out that in the first 3 questions they looked at what Jesus did. Now they will examine what He expects His disciples (us) to do.

Jesus commanded His disciples to **"make disciples of all nations."** Just as the disciples had learned from Him, the nations were to become Jesus' disciples through them. As Jesus' disciples today, He commands *us* to **"make disciples of all nations" (Matt. 28:19).**

5. A witness describes what he or she has experienced. We are therefore to witness to the world what we have experienced in Jesus Christ. This includes our experience in His Word as well as His experience in our lives.

6. A good witness will truthfully and cheerfully give such information wherever the opportunity arises. An ineffective witness will clam up or give a false testimony in word and deed.

7. Paul calls our witnessing **"the ministry of reconciliation" (2 Cor. 5:18).** Emphasize that reconciliation brings two warring parties together in peace. When we share the Gospel, we, in a sense, bring God and sinful human beings together.

8. An ambassador is a ruler's personal representative to a foreign country. We represent Christ to the world.

9. The term *ambassador of reconciliation* seems appropriate at this point. Such an ambassador certainly can––and at times must––act alone. But that's not the design God

gives to His "called-out ones." We have a responsibility to do mission work together (e.g., as a congregation, District, or synod) in addition to the individual obligations we still have. God calls us to both "witness where we are" and, at the same time, to participate in the more widespread mission of the organized church.

PRACTICE (Objectives 3––4)
This activity is based on **Titus 2.** Use this section to show how each believer can make a strong witness to his or her Lord in everyday situations.

Begin by reading **Titus 2** together. Show how Paul includes all age groups and types as witnesses. Then have each student independently write one example of how the type named can be a witness to the Lord through the situation given.

1. Older men:
a. With temperance and self control.
b. Be fair, faithful, forgiving, as God is.
c. Practice the lessons you have learned.
d. Don't let anger turn to hatred.
2. Older women:
a. Speak truthfully, as fellow members.
b. Submit as to Christ, out of love.
c. Give children training and instruction of the Lord.
3. Younger men:
a. Control passions and sexual desires.
b. Be motivated by love for Christ.
c. Speak as God would.
4. Employees:
a. Serve as if the Lord were your supervisor.
b. Give honor and respect to those over you.
c. Put up with others, forgiving them.

Much discussion may result. These examples may seem way out of step with the time. Remind students to make their goal the same as the goal Paul gave to Titus: to give the best picture of Christ to the world.

WRAP-UP
Close with an oral reading of Phil. 4:4–9.

Session 10: Concluding Activities
for Units 1-2

To help students remember terms, concepts, etc., that you have taught, you will need to provide review opportunites from time to time. If you wish, you can also use these review exercises to help you evaluate your teaching and your students' learning.

You may use the material that follows for these purposes. As you do, remember that classes and students vary. Therefore you will need to adapt these suggestions to fit your class and your students. Always review or test concepts you covered in class, even if they differ from those that appear here or in the corresponding Student Book pages.

To complete the suggested review activities, students will need to reread and rethink each session title as a means of focusing on major concepts, assimilate vocabulary as a way of establishing a foundation of terminology, reread and search for key concepts in Bible references already studied, be able to formulate key understandings in their own words (as opposed to memorizing or parroting textual expressions), and organize lists of data.

Concentrate on a review rather than on memorizing facts to prepare for a test. A well-written test can, however, serve the following purposes:

1. Organize key concepts, facts, and understandings

2. Force the students to think and organize

3. Provide an opportunity for a third review (when you review the test itself after you have corrected it)

4. Give each student some idea of his or her success in mastering the material

This review is intended for use in one class period. Some activities may be done individually. Others could be done more profitably as a class or small-group activity.

The Student Book activities for session 10 are designed to help students prepare for the evaluation activity you will provide.

VOCABULARY:

Match the definition or identification with the correct term or name.

Part 1

A. Ambassador	F. Heresy
B. Cornerstone	G. Reconcile
C. Create	H. Sacrament
D. Ecclesia	I. Saints
E. Grace	J. Witness

1. (I) The faithful in Christ Jesus
2. (E) Undeserved kindness from God
3. (D) Greek for "called-out ones"
4. (C) To make from nothing
5. (B) Most important foundation stone
6. (F) False doctrine
7. (H) An act of God that creates faith and forgives sins, using His Word and physical means
8. (J) One who tells what he or she has experienced
9. (A) One who officially represents his or her ruler
10. (G) To bring warring parties together

Part 2

A. Baptism	I. Gifts of the Spirit
B. Body of Christ	J. Gospel
C. Christ	K. Holy Communion
D. Church	L. Jesus
E. Colossian Christians	M. Paul
F. Epaphras	N. Roman Christians
G. Ephesus	O. Titus
H. Fruit of the Spirit	

1. (M) The last of the apostles to be chosen
2. (C) The Anointed One, the Messiah
3. (L) Savior
4. (F) A Christian from Colossae
5. (N) Paul was encouraged by their faith
6. (A) Sacrament that uses water and the Word
7. (K) Sacrament in which Christ gives us His body and blood

8. (O) A coworker of Paul; a "troubleshooter"
9. (E) Group bothered by false teaching, recipients of one of Paul's letters
10. (G) Location of Temple of Diana
11. (J) The good news of salvation in Christ
12. (D) The name of Jesus' "called-out ones"
13. (H) Signs of Christ in a person
14. (I) Special gifts received by members of the church
15. (B) Paul's analogy to illustrate the church

KEY CONCEPTS

Reread the material suggested. Then answer the questions.

1. **Session 1: Eph. 1:3–14.** Explain how this list of seven actions by God can make a "called-out one" more confident of salvation.

(God does each of these for believers. Since His promises are sure, we can be confident that He does them for each of us.)

2. **Session 1:** List four characteristics of (a) church— "community of called-out ones" and four of (b) church—congregation, organization, denomination.

("Community of called-out ones": members do not know who belongs; God chose members from eternity; members joined at baptism; Christ is the real Leader.)

(Congregation, organization, denomination: members have name on a roster; contains hypocrites; sometime owns property; led by a member of the clergy.)

3. **Session 2: Col. 1:1–14.** Describe two ways God uses people to bring the Gospel to others.

(God uses people to bring the Gospel to others by preaching and teaching [e.g., Epaphras, Paul] and by the example of their lives to others [e.g., the Colossians].)

4. **Session 3: Eph. 2:1–18.** Why can conversion be called a miracle of God?

(In conversion God revives a completely dead, contrary, spiritual nature. The owner has absolutely no power to assist—or even to accept. It is God's work entirely.)

5. **Session 4: Eph. 2:19–22.** How is the church like an ancient temple?

(The church is founded on the foundation of the apostles and prophets. Jesus Christ is the Cornerstone. Each member becomes a living stone in the building itself.)

6. **Session 5:** How is the human body an excellent picture of the church?

(The human body is controlled by the head. Jesus Christ is the Head of His body, the church. All parts work under His control and for the growth of all.)

7. **Session 6: Rom. 1:11–13.** How can "called-out ones" today encourage and strengthen each other's faith?

(They can encourage and strengthen each other by sharing the Gospel with one another in Word and Sacrament and by "living" the Gospel in their daily lives.)

8. **Session 7: 1 Tim. 4.** How is God's Word like food?

(God's Word nourishes and strengthens. It must be consumed regularly. Its power is given by God, its Author. It is distributed by God's representatives to a hungry and thirsty world.)

9. **Session 8: Matt. 28:16–20, 1 Cor. 11:23–26.** Explain Baptism to a 5-year-old. Explain Holy Communion to a newly converted native of New Guinea.
(Answers will vary and should be interesting.)

10. **Session 9: John 3:16–18.** Write what God the Father could have said to Jesus to describe and explain what He would have to do to redeem humanity.

(These answers will also vary. If possible, allow time to share them with the class.)

LISTS

1. Seven actions of God in redeeming us (Blessing, choosing, predestining, redeeming, forgiving, instructing, gathering)
2. Eight fruits of the Spirit (Love, joy, patience, kindness, goodness, faithfulness, gentleness, self-control)
3. Three parts of God's eternal temple (Foundation of apostles and prophets [Scripture], Cornerstone [Christ], living stones [members])

4. Eight gifts of the Spirit to the church (Apostles, prophets, teachers, miracle workers, healers, helpers, administrators, speakers in tongues)
5. Ten ways of telling the Good News (Answers will vary.)
6. The two sacraments of the Lutheran Church (Holy Baptism and Holy Communion)

Unit 3: Worship, the Church's Breath

Having studied in general what the church is and what it does, we are now ready to look more deeply into each aspect of its life. Worship is basic to this life, just as living organisms must rely on respiration.

We will begin by seeing that God is always the center of worship, but that in the church all members need to do it together. The two major directions of worship (sacrament and sacrifice) provide an opportunity for your class to practice their spiritual respiration in a worship service.

Begin immediately to plan this activity so it can be one in which students experience the true value of worship.

Session 11: Centering Worship

BIBLE BASIS: 1 Cor. 10:1–13

CENTRAL TRUTH

God has redeemed us. Now He demands and empowers us to make Him the center of our worship.

OBJECTIVES

That the students will
1. define worship;
2. tell how to recognize when worship is carried on;
3. relate how God should be the center of true worship because He has created, redeemed, and sanctified us;
4. tell how we sin when we replace God with something else as the center of worship;
5. express confidence in the ability God gives them to use the power of the Gospel to defeat temptation.

BACKGROUND

Unit 3 takes up the subject of worship. Worship is one of the most characteristic activities of the church. In these five sessions the students will be led to define worship and to see how as individuals they practice it. This concept will then be expanded to include corporate worship. Finally, students will be asked to use **these concepts in a worship service** they conduct. Alert the class to this upcoming activity.

The warnings from God in 1 Cor. 10:1–13 are, of course, statements of Law. Let God's law speak to your students. But do not neglect to speak the Gospel also. God had shown His grace to Israel, and He continues to show it to us today. Part of this Gospel message comes in **verse 13**, where Paul assures us that God always provides a way out so we can stand up under temptation.

Pray that the power of the Gospel will move every student in your class to center his or her worship on Christ.

STRETCHING (Objectives 1--2)

Make this activity an integral part of the lesson. Use it to help students see what worship is. Each activity pictures a kind of worship. For example, the person washing the car is worshiping the car by the acts of washing, drying, and polishing.

Perhaps, for further clarification, the students can provide activities, objects, and acts of worship in their lives. Emphasize that everyone worships in this wide definition sense. **Be sure to point out then that the chief object of worship in a person's life is that which is worth the most to him or her. God demands that we make Him that center of worship.**

GETTING THE WORD (Objectives 3--5)

The reading in **1 Cor. 10** demonstrates St. Paul's knowledge of Old Testament history. For your students this session will provide an excellent opportunity to review some Old Testament events.

Verses 1–5

Read the Student Book material together. Then assign selected students to read and report briefly on the Old Testament events. Finally, discuss the questions that follow.

1. Paul compares the crossing of the Red Sea with Holy Baptism. In both instances God was acting graciously to give new life to sinful human beings. Both require faith in His promises. Both give freedom, delivering from the power of an enemy (Pharaoh and Satan). Seeing this demonstration of God's pure grace should fill students with gratitude and move them to place God at the center of life.

2. St. John shows how Christ is the heavenly bread that comes down from heaven **(John 6:35–59).** While these words extend beyond Holy Communion, they also foreshadow this sacrament, in which Christ comes to each of us personally, to forgive our sins and strengthen our faith. He makes the first move to be the center of our lives.

3. Unlike all other religions, worship in Christianity is a reaction to God's grace. We dare not hope to gain any reward or merit because of our worship. Christ has already won our reward.

Verses 6–10

The opposite of worship is sin. In the following examples the two questions presented could be answered as follows:
1. Ex. 32:1–6
   a. The golden calf--a symbol of Israel's pride
   b. Its construction; eating, drinking, and dancing.
2. **Num.** 25:1–18
   a. Sexual pleasure; self-gratification
   b. Immorality with the Moabites
3. **Num.** 21:4–9

   a. Self; knowing more than God
   b. Grumbling and complaining
4. **Num.** 16:41–50
   a. Self-righteousness; accusing God of being unfair
   b. Criticism of God and His representatives

Verses 11–13

1. The self-righteous, self-confident person is ripe for a fall. This happened, for example, to Peter, who promised Christ that he would never disown Him **(Mark 14:27–31).**

2. **Verse 13** speaks of the power of the Gospel. Because of the love for Christ that the Holy Spirit has given us, we have the power to defeat Satan's temptations.

3. Use this as a time to share experiences, but not to brag. Lead students to praise the power of God.

PRACTICE (Objectives 1--5)

In the examples given, true worship and false worship (sin) could be seen as follows:

Worship

a. praise God; hear His Word
b. share with needy; honor God
c. cheer friend; express concern
d. use talent for God's glory
e. want to talk to God
f. be a good team member
g. hear God's word

Replacement

a. hear gossip; fulfill a class requirement
b. do something because everyone is doing it; show off
c. retain person as a friend
d. get compliments for self
e. want to get something for self
f. humiliate defender; show off
g. punishment for not listening; reward for doing so

2. This activity can be a written homework assignment. If students do not wish to share with the class, have them turn their papers in to you. Assure them of confidentiality. In either case, you should be able to see how well students grasp the importance of God in their lives.

WRAP-UP

Collect ideas for a prayer in which you collectively ask for nothing for self but only for things that honor God and further His kingdom.

Session 12: Sharing Worship

BIBLE BASIS: 1 Cor. 14:26—33

CENTRAL TRUTH

In God-pleasing worship, individuals edify one another. For this to happen, individuals need to cooperate with others in the group. At times we may need to lay aside our own worship preferences for the good of the congregation of "called-out ones."

OBJECTIVES

That the students will

1. identify differences between private and corporate worship;

2. describe practices that unify and some that disrupt corporate worship;

3. tell how corporate worship builds up the faith of each worshiper.

BACKGROUND

In this session we begin the emphasis of the role of a congregation in the church. We will examine the importance of corporate worship in the lives of individual believers.

This session also borders on potentially controversial subjects: the role of women in the church (**1 Cor. 14:33—36**) and speaking in tongues (**1 Cor. 12—14**). Try to avoid becoming sidetracked on these doctrines. If questions arise, deal with them as honestly and lovingly as you can. Consult a good commentary for help. Also read recent documents on those topics from the Commission on Theology and Church Relations of The Lutheran Church—Missouri Synod.

STRETCHING (Objectives 1 and 3)

This fictional story illustrates the importance of corporate worship. A believer's faith and its exercise may soon grow cold when another's faith is not shared.

GETTING THE WORD: 1 Cor. 14:26—33 (Objectives 1-3)

After discussing the role of speaking in tongues, which apparently had caused dissension, Paul moved on to the matter of corporate worship. There had also been problems here, when individuals had insisted on their right to speak or lead. Obviously a lack of love for the Lord and for each other was at the bottom of the problem.

We have no detailed information on the conduct of early Christian services. Especially among gentile Christians, there was no set order. Jewish Christians at least had the tradition of the synagogue to form a framework.

1. It seems that as each worshiper exercised his or her particular gift, confusion sometimes resulted. Encourage students to speculate what such a service may have been like.

2. The lack of order probably came from their eagerness to lead. Such eagerness was another symptom of sinful pride, which rears its ugly head even among "called-out ones."

3. Such services might become shouting matches. See also 1 Cor. 1:10—12 and 1 Cor. 11:17—22.

4. Following the predictable results of such contests, the loudest, strongest, and most influential probably had their way. This was hardly an example of Christian love.

5. Before you discuss this question, be sure everyone thoroughly understands the definitions of private and corporate worship.

As Paul states in **1 Cor. 14:26b**, corporate worship should always lead to *edification*. Draw special attention to this word, since it does not appear in the Student Book. You may define *edification* as "the strengthening of the church through the means of grace."

6. In order to edify, only revelations that are understood have value. This might say something about the practice of singing or "performing" in a foreign language for art's sake in worship services today.

7. Christian love would dictate that the "special delivery message" would

get preference over one that had been in progress. We must understand that in those days people did not have the New Testament portion of the Bible. Perhaps for this reason the Holy Spirit must have often provided "live revelations." Now that we have the entire canon, the Holy Spirit works through that Word instead of through such "special deliveries."

8. Paul was primarily concerned about the Gospel. God presents a Gospel of peace—peace through Christ. Why, then, should "called-out ones" live and worship with dissension?

PRACTICE (Objectives 2—3)

1. All these common excuses have a common denominator, sinful pride. They view worship as a means of "getting something." According to our definition true worship occurs only when the worshiper does something to respond to God's love. The excuses also show a lack of love toward fellow believers.

2. The unity described in **Acts 4:32–35** grew from a unity of motivation: the grace of God. It showed itself in a desire to return love and devotion to God through showing love and concern for one another.

3. Following are possible corporate worship activities that would equate with the private worship acts.

> The public Confession of Sins
> Congregational singing
> Listening to the sermon
> The sacraments

4. All the acts listed give to the corporate worshiper the feeling of being among winners. As Paul mentioned in **Rom. 1:12**, we are encouraged by each other's faith, something that cannot happen alone. Develop the emotional response of each activity. Share your own feelings as you remember them. Encourage the sharing of personal experiences, at Christmas, confirmation, Easter, etc.

WRAP-UP

A natural way to conclude this session would be for the class to stand in a circle, look at each other with confidence, and say the Apostles' Creed in firm voices.

Session 13: Receiving in Worship

BIBLE BASIS: 1 Tim. 1:12–17; 2 Tim. 3:14–17; Matt. 26:26–28; Acts 2:38–39

CENTRAL TRUTH

In corporate worship, God gives us His grace in the acts we call sacramental. They include the forgiveness of sins, hearing His Word, and receiving the sacraments.

OBJECTIVES

That the students will

1. describe the difference between sacramental and sacrificial acts;

2. summarize Jesus' requirements for worship, the rationale of liturgical worship, and major developments in "the mass";

3. demonstrate that they understand the significance of three sacramental acts: absolution, the Word, and the sacraments.

BACKGROUND

The format of this session differs from previous sessions. You will begin by introducing a concept. Students will then read factual material and related Scripture passages. Finally, they will answer questions about the material. Explain and illustrate the concept in "Stretching." Then fill an advisory role. The Student Book contains the background material usually found here.

During this session you may have time to begin planning the worship service suggested for session 15. See **"Looking Ahead"** at the end of this session for some suggestions.

Pray that the Holy Spirit will use the Word as presented in this session to enrich the liturgical worship experiences of the students in your class.

STRETCHING (Objective 1)

Most sophomores have had biology or are taking it now. Therefore they should be able to understand the analogy between respiration and worship. The Holy Spirit is sometimes referred to as the "Breath of God."

Animals need to take in oxygen and exhale carbon dioxide. When the church inhales, it takes in God's grace. This happens during sacramental acts of worship. When it exhales, it returns to God its love and devotion (in sacrifical acts of worship).

An animal that would only take in oxygen would soon die from a buildup of carbon dioxide. It would also die if it could not inhale oxygen. Similarly, the church becomes stagnant and self-centered if it only takes in God's grace and never returns it with acts of love or devotion. And just so a church that only "does things" and never bothers to inhale God's grace, soon becomes a mere social club.

GETTING THE WORD   (Objectives 2--3)
The Student Book contains the essential information for this section.

PRACTICE   (Objective 3)
Following are possible for answers to Student Book questions. Plan to discuss and evaluate them during session 14.
1. See notes above for "Stretching."
2. Sacramental: Acts in worship in which God gives the church His grace.
   Sacrifical: Acts in worship in which the church gives to God its love and devotion.
3. Jesus requires only that we worship Him in spirit and in truth.
4. Christians use many ways to worship because God did not command any set form.
5. Liturgical worship provides a balance of sacramental and sacrifical acts of worship, a set framework that allows necessary variations, and a link with the church of the Old Testament.
6. "Mass" is a shortened version of the priest's final word, "You are dismissed."
7. Martin Luther retained the main framework of the Mass. He eliminated parts contrary to Scripture and gave worshipers more of an active role, as in singing.
8. The three sacramental activities are absolution (God forgives our sins), the readings and sermon (God gives us

His Word) and the Sacraments (Holy Baptism and Holy Communion).
9. We cannot approach God with love or devotion until the barrier of sin has been removed. Only God, through the atoning sacrifice of Christ, can do this.
10. Hearing God's Word thoroughly equips us for every good work by teaching, rebuking, correcting, and training us in righteousness.
11. In receiving the true body and blood of Christ, we personally partake in His life in us. It is indeed a personal, spiritual, and physical meeting.
12. (Not discussed in this session; students should be able to make some conclusions.) Through Baptism God brings His grace to a new believer. The entire congregation can be edified by sharing this joyous occasion, and the baptized person can be blessed by the prayers and commitments of the congregation.

LOOKING AHEAD
Begin making plans now for the class worship in session 15. Following are some important considerations.
1. Decide on the service to be used and the worship resources available. Consider such things as hymnal, provision for music, space, and personnel.
2. Strongly consider the use of the divine service used during Sunday worship. This will help students see both sacramental and sacrifical elements. Since you will not invite an entire congregation to your service, do not plan to celebrate Holy Communion.
3. Approach this activity as a serious occasion. Choose leaders on the basis of ability and not popularity. Try to involve as many as possible in special roles. For example:
   Presiding minister: Read Gospel, preach.
   Assistant ministers: Offer prayers, read liturgy.
   Readers: Read Old Testament and Epistle readings.
   Acolytes: Light candles.
   Musicians: Play organ, piano, portable keyboard, or guitar; sing the propers.

Ushers: Receive offering.
Arrangements: Set up and take down.
4. Practice sessions are entirely in order. Remind everyone, however, that pleasing an audience is not the goal of the worship. Encourage them to do their best for the Lord and His people, and not to seek good reviews for themselves.
5. Use part of this session to begin formulating your plans.

Session 14: Giving in Worship

BIBLE BASIS: Col. 3:15-17; 1 Tim. 2:1-8; 2 Cor. 8:1-7

CENTRAL TRUTH
In corporate worship, the Holy Spirit empowers us to return to God our love through songs, prayers, and offerings. We call these the sacrifical acts of worship.

OBJECTIVES
That the students will
1. identify the difference between sacramental and sacrifical acts of worship;
2. tell how the Old Testament sacrifice serves as a basis for our sacrifical gifts;
3. list three criteria necessary for an act of worship to be called sacrifical;
4. evaluate present day worship acts on the basis of these three criteria.

BACKGROUND
This session logically follows the discussion of sacramental acts during session 13. As you discuss sacrifical acts, emphasize that our actions grow out of God's grace; they don't cause it.

Use some of this session's time to plan and practice for the worship experience in session 15.

Students should have in hand the hymnal you will use. (We recommend *Lutheran Worship* or *The Lutheran Hymnal*.)

If necessary, postpone **Practice 2** for another time. At the time you discuss this activity, you should allow plenty of time for students to express their feelings.

Pray that the Holy Spirit will move your students to respond to His grace with songs, prayers, and offerings.

STRETCHING (Objective 1)
Talk about student answers to the questions from **"Practice"** in session 13. Consider asking students to exchange papers and to evaluate and correct another's work. After everyone has finished, the partners could meet and discuss how and why they marked the answers. Be sure to allow time for class discussion of answers where students disagree.

Make the transition to the subject of exhaling in respiration and its parallel in sacrifical acts of worship.

GETTING THE WORD (Objectives 2-3)

Sacrificial Worship
1. Help students see the connection between sacrificial worship and Old Testament sacrifices. Correct the notion that a sacrifice is "when you give up a lot." Rather, stress the summary statements in the Student Book.
2. These three criteria are based on the following New Testament examples:
   1 John 4:19: The act results from God's grace to us.
   2 Cor. 9:6-7: The act is a voluntary action from us to God.
   Matt. 25:34-40: The act is always directed to God or to others.
3. The three catagories listed often overlap, and are listed this way for the sake of discussion. Be sure to stress that even though God demands our gifts, He does not need them. We need to give them as an exercise of faith. Faith without works (exercise, exhaling) soon dies.

What Does God Say?
Take the necessary time and effort to clarify the references listed. Allow the students to decide which

words fit each criterion. Encourage discussion and allow variation. The following could be correct responses.

Songs: Col. 3:15-17
a. "peace of Christ" (v. 15)
b. "with gratitude in your hearts" (v. 16)
c. "to God" (v. 16 or 17)

Prayers: 1 Tim. 2:1-8
a. "who gave Himself as a ransom for all men" (v. 6)
b. "without anger or disputing" (v. 8)
c. "pleases God our Savior" (v. 3) "for kings and all those in authority" (v. 2)

Offerings: 2 Cor. 8:1-7
a. "the grace that God has given" (v. 1)
b. "welled up in rich generosity" (v. 2)
c. "gave themselves first to the Lord" (v. 5)

PRACTICE (Objective 4)
1. Use your hymnal to help explain these parts of the service. Following are suggested answers:

Introit
a. Absolution
b. God
c. Song (psalm)

Kyrie
a. Promise of mercy
b. God
c. Prayer

Hymn of Praise ("Gloria" or "This Is the Feast")
a. Absolution
b. God
c. Song

Sermon Hymn
a. Hearing the Word
b. God, others
c. Song

Offertory
a. Hearing the Word
b. God
c. Song

Offering
a. Hearing the Word
b. God, others
c. Gift

Prayers
a. Hearing the Word
b. God
c. Prayer

Agnus Dei
a. Sacrament
b. Jesus Christ
c. Song

Post-Communion Hymn
a. Sacrament
b. God
c. Song

2. The acts listed are only the beginning of a list of practices carried out in local worship settings. Use the three criteria listed as the basis for evaluation. Notice that "we've always done this" is not one of them. No effort is made here to evaluate this list. Each should be judged on its own merits and in its own setting.

WRAP-UP
Practice and/or discuss the upcoming worship experience. Perhaps you could explain the benediction and then pronounce it.

Session 15: Worshiping

CENTRAL TRUTH
When we worship, we receive God's grace and offer our praise, prayers, and gifts to Him.

OBJECTIVES
That the student will
1. experience the joy of worship;
2. evaluate that experience.

BACKGROUND
Plan to devote most of this class period to the worship experience. As much as possible, have arrangements, materials, and other items ready before the class arrives. You might appoint a committee to handle these arrangements. Help them make as many preparations as possible during the preceding periods.

Pray that this experience will uplift students and will also help them "get more out of" worship experiences in their congregations.

STRETCHING (Objective 1)
The rubrics presented here are of a general nature and reflect worship customs among Lutherans for many years.

Review them before the service.

GETTING THE WORD (Objective 1)

The readings chosen for this service are the vehicle for the Word in this session. If someone presents a short sermon, he should base it on one of these readings.

PRACTICE (Objective 2)

Have the students answer the Students Book questions immediately after the service. They should write their responses on a separate sheet of paper. Consider using these reflections in one of these ways:

1. Students hand in their reflections anonymously.

2. Students discuss their thoughts in groups.

3. Students and teacher share orally what has been written.

If you hear or read reactions, they will help you evaluate the effectiveness of the experience. Consider these points:

1. How seriously did they consider this experience?

2. How conscientious were those who had leadership roles?

3. What level of participation was evident?

4. What did you consider the most effective part? What was the least effective? Does you opinion agree with the consensus of the class?

5. If your class conducts another service, what could be done to remedy ineffective parts?

Be sure to emphasize the positive aspects of the experience. Negative aspects should be mentioned in the spirit of constructive criticism.

Worship flies in the face of existing customs related to social and entertainment gatherings. Unless your class has a deep tradition of corporate worship, you may feel discouraged by a low level of participation or by behavior problems. Continue to look for opportunities to "teach" worship. Also consider doing another service later in the year, profiting from the pluses and minuses of this one.

Unit 4: Growth, the Church's Life

Now that the church is seen as a special gathering of "called-out ones," the students are ready to see the church at work in a local congregation.

Activities in this unit should provide opportunities for students to observe the signs of growth in a Christian congregation as the Spirit creates faith, nurtures it, and protects it against its enemies.

In this unit we will examine the miracle of how a congregation begins and grows. Students will be asked to prepare a short report on the history of their congregation. The first four sessions will present topics to research. You will need to decide on deadlines, format, and possible class use of the research. This activity is, of course, an option, but it could become an important part of the course.

Also, we encourage you to invite a local pastor to speak to the class on the work of the ministry within a congregation.

Throughout unit 4 emphasize that the Spirit is at work in the local congregation, a visible evidence of the church.

Session 16: Planting the Seed

BIBLE BASIS: 2 Tim. 1:3-12

CENTRAL TRUTH

The church exists in the gatherings of the "called-out ones," called congregations. God caused such congregations to be formed by hearers who received the Gospel and, through the Holy Spirit, believed it.

OBJECTIVES

That the students will

1. compare the growth of a plant with the growth of a congregation;

2. tell how a congregation begins when the Gospel is preached, believed, and practiced by a group of like-minded believers;

3. describe how this process has operated in the history of their local congregations.

BACKGROUND

What is a congregation? How many people does it take to make a congregation? What else is necessary? While God gives us some guidelines for congregational worship, He does not provide a definition of the term. Jesus does tell us, though, that **"where two or three come together in My name, there am I with them"** (Matt. 18:20). Timothy, his mother, and his grandmother certainly formed a type of congregation (2 Tim. 1:5), just as we can consider a Christian family today to be a congregation. Beyond this, the laying on of hands **(v. 6)** suggests that Timothy was part of a larger congregation.

During this session we shall propose three marks of any Christian congregation: Someone speaks the Gospel, someone hears the Word, and the Holy Spirit creates and strengthens faith.

Pray that the Holy Spirit will fill your students as they hear God's Word in class, in their homes, and in their local congregations.

STRETCHING (Objective 1)

The crossword puzzle will provide both a change of pace and a means to suggest the concept of plant growth as an analogy to church growth. The correct answers are are based on the New International Version of the Bible, but students using other translations should easily be able to complete most of it. Following are the answers:

Across	Down
1. GRASS	2. RUE
4. WORD	3. BREAD
5. ELIM	4. WORRIES
8. APOLLOS	6. LILIES
10. FIG	7. MUSTARD
11. VINE	9. OLIVE
12. WEED	

GETTING THE WORD (Objective 2)

As you study **2 Tim. 1:3—12,** emphasize how the Gospel is the motivation for the formation of a congregation.

1. The sketchy information from this section indicates only that Timothy was first exposed to the Gospel through his grandmother, Lois, and his mother, Eunice. This gathering of three certainly is the nucleus of a congregation. Also note that in the family parents feed and guide the children and each other.

2. God provides spiritual leadership for believing families and, through the Holy Spirit, sends His representatives to begin such congregations.

Timothy's leadership **(v. 6)** began when Paul laid his hands on him (ordination), setting him apart as a special ambassador of Christ.

Paul's ordination **(v. 11)** occurred when Christ Himself set him apart as a special messenger to the gentiles **(Acts 9:15)**

3. The words of **2 Tim.1:9—10** are one of Paul's finest summaries of the Gospel. Spend time reviewing the emphasis on pure grace in our salvation. Note our complete passivity and God's complete activity.

4. The formula presented here is merely a way of dramatizing God's active role in our salvation and in the formation of a congregation. The following are the possible answers to the activity:

John 20:19—23

a. **"Peace be with you"** (vv. 19 and 21)

b. Christ

c. The disciples

d. **"He breathed on them and said, 'Receive the Holy Spirit'"** (v. 22)

e. The apostles

Acts 2:14—41

a. **"Repent and be baptized, every one of you, in the name of Jesus Christ for the forgiveness of your sins"**

b. Pet

c. **"Men of Israel"** (v. 22)

d. **"Those who accepted his message were baptized."** (v. 41)

e. The Jerusalem church

Acts 10:24—48

a. **"Everyone who believes in Him receives forgiveness of sins"** (v.

43)
b. Peter
c. Gentiles
d. **"They heard them speaking in tongues and praising God" (v. 46)**
e. Household of Cornelius
Acts 19:1-7
a. **"He told the people to believe . . . in Jesus" (v. 4)**
b. Paul
c. Ephesians
d. **"They spoke in tongues" (v. 6)**
e. Ephesian congregation
5. Answers for the analogy: Seed = Word of God; farmer = Gospel witness; Soil = hearers; heat and moisture = work of Holy Spirit; germination = miracle of faith in hearer's hearts.

PRACTICE (Objective 3)

In order to differentiate "church" (communion of saints) from "church" (local congregation or physical group of professed believers), we will call the latter a congregation.

The report suggested here is intended to make the students conscious of the Holy Spirit's work in their lives, particularly in their congregations. You will need to decide how and when this report should be done. Consider differing backgrounds, abilities, and time limitations. As you plan, consider the following:

1. Students should do the work outside of class.

2. You need to establish definite parameters (length, format, oral or written, deadlines, etc.).

3. If some students are not members of a congregation, assign them to one near their home.

4. Take advantage of the subject matter that requires research rather than "xeroxing facts from the library."

5. Alert local pastors to the possible contacts they can make with your students.

6. Set realistic deadlines, but don't allow too much time to elapse (certainly not more than three weeks).

WRAP-UP

Form a prayer circle and pray for your school's administrators. Consider them as the Holy Spirit's messengers of the Gospel to your school.

Session 17: Nurturing the Crop

BIBLE BASIS: 2 Tim. 2:1-10

CENTRAL TRUTH

God instructs and empowers the members of the church to proclaim the Gospel to each other and to the world.

OBJECTIVES

That the students will

1. tell how God's grace serves as the motivation for the existence of a congregation;

2. identify the proclamation of the Gospel as the primary goal of a congregation;

3. share some ways proclaiming the Gospel can be hard and dangerous work;

4. tell why goals other than those indicated by the Lord are not acceptable for a congregation.

BACKGROUND

Ask a local pastor to be a guest of your class for this session. **Be sure to make arrangements for his** presentation in plenty of time for him to prepare. His purpose: to make real the work of proclaiming the Gospel. Before his presentation, the class should study 2 Tim. 2:1-10.

The pastor should make his presentation and answer questions at the beginning of **"Practice."**

As you read the various instructions Paul gives, you may be struck by the fact that again and again he provides a Gospel context and motivation for these instructions. Look for opportunities to highlight this fact as you discuss 2 Tim. 2:1-10 with your class. Pray that the Holy Spirit will fill your students with that motivation for their lives.

STRETCHING (Objectives 2 and 4)

These four descriptions introduce what many congregations strive to become. In a world that seeks to be able to measure success, these four organizations often become models for congregations to follow.

Allow discussion to flow as students try to identify which organization comes the closest to a congregations's real purpose. Perhaps the school would be closest, since its educational goal would be somewhat similar to the goal of a congregation: to proclaim the Gospel (a type of education).

GETTING THE WORD (Objectives 1, 2–3)

These words, addressed to Timothy, **provide instructions for a congregation** today. Both a pastor and a congregation receive the same grace of God and have the same mandate: to make disciples of all nations by preaching and baptizing.

Verses 1–2

1. We are strong in God's grace when we are confident of His love for us in Christ and confidently display that love to each other and to the world. An individual or a congregation can do this only when Christ lives in and through them.

2. This grace of God (the Gospel) should be entrusted to those who believe it and practice it. Notice the care with which Christ trained His disciples and how concerned Paul was about those who preached the Gospel (2 Cor. 11:1–15).

3. God calls on congregations to proclaim the Gospel to each other and to the world (2 Tim. 2:2). Whatever else a congregation does, it must primarily seek to accomplish this.

Verses 3–7

Just proclaiming the Gospel will cause strong reactions. Satan, the world, and our own human nature will sometimes react violently to God's free gift of salvation. To illustrate this, Paul uses examples of three occupations.

1. The hardships of a soldier include loneliness, threat of injury and death, and the temptations to become sidetracked. This last hardship would include longing for home and for freedom from military discipline, and the temptation to go AWOL. But good soldiers stay with it because of loyalty to their commander and, ultimately, their country. Satan also

tempts Christian "soldiers" to look back at the old life of sin and self-gratification. Love for Christ empowers us to resist those temptations and to "stay with it."

2. Athletes must obey rules of training and of the sport. If they break training or disregard the rules of the game, they are disqualified. Jesus' rules are simple: Out of love to Him, use your talents (2 Tim. 2:15–16), and do it with love (1 John 4:7–12). This holds true for a congregation also.

3. Farmers, besides selling their crop, also use it for their own sustenance. Similarly the congregation, while "giving away the Gospel," also lives on it. We delight in the pay we receive: Seeing the Gospel change lives, (for example, when the fruit of the Spirit [Gal. 5:22–23] is evident in the congregation).

Verses 8–10

1. "I endure everything for the sake of the elect, that they too may obtain the salvation that is in Christ Jesus" (2 Tim. 2:10)

2. This goal is to "save" as many as possible. "Save" here means that, through the congregation's proclamation of the Word, people will believe the Gospel.

3. See "Stretching."

PRACTICE (Objectives 1–4)

1. Use this outside speaker as an opportunity to reinforce the objectives already stated. Give a copy of this session to the pastor before his appearance. The Student Book suggests some topics to be discussed.

2. Use this as a supplement to or substitute for the pastor's visit. You could do this in groups. Each group would make a report, outlining their program and emphasizing their goals. Some reports will be ridiculous, but they may come close to what some congregations do in the name of religion.

3. Add these questions to the outline of the report. Explain, if necessary, how and where students can obtain this information. Be sure everyone understands that to get a quote (d), they will have to talk

personally with their pastor.

WRAP-UP
One or two students could close the

Session 18: Guarding Against Pests

BIBLE BASIS: 2 Tim. 2:14—4:5

CENTRAL TRUTH
Satan attacks members of
congregations with temptations and
troubles. Using the power of God as
revealed in His Word, we can fight off
these attacks.

OBJECTIVES
That the students will
1. compare plant-growth problems to
troubles Satan brings to congregations;
2. categorize various temptations
and describe God's antidote for each;
3. suggest solutions to these
troubles;
4. identify selected problems in
their congregations, along with
proposed solutions to these problems.

BACKGROUND
High-school students tend to
minimize the dangers we face because of
Satan. Compared to most adults, they
have limited experience in recognizing
him and his techniques. Therefore they
often regard warning from adults as
middle-age fears and signs of old age.
To counteract this tendency, this
session compares garden pests to
Satan's handiwork. Some of the
terminology might seem humorous, but
the intention is not. If the use of
this terminology helps prepare our
young warriors to recognize and battle
the enemy, the exaggerations have
accomplished their purpose.
Pray that your students will take
seriously the temptations Paul
describes in the text, as well as other
temptations with which Satan approaches
them today. Ask God to cause them to
turn to Him for power to resist those
temptations, using the power He offers
in His "cure," His "repellent," and His
"real care company."

STRETCHING (Objective 1)
Spend just enough time with this

analogy for students to understand it.
The garden pests (disease, insect,
animal and human) were chosen because
they roughly parallel Paul's
presentation in our text.

GETTING THE WORD (Objective 2)
The reading 2 Tim. 2:14—4:5 is
longer than usual. It contains
excellent descriptions of the enemies
of the church. Paul was warning his
young friend, Timothy, what problems he
would face. Paul also, again and
again, repeated God's answer to each
problem. Note that each solution
centers in the power of the Gospel--the
grace of God in Jesus Christ. In all
the discussion and in the roleplaying
that follows, be sure to come back to
this ground of faith.

2 Tim. 2:14-19
The two diseases described here are
distortions of the Word. How often the
church has argued, disagreed, and
parted company over meanings of words!
Too often only sinful pride--not
truth--is at stake.
The second pest can be just as
insidious, especially among active
Christians. Just having a seminar,
meeting, lecture, a class, or a concert
doesn't mean that the Gospel is being
proclaimed. The Gospel must be the
center, or it is simply "chatter."
God proclaims the Gospel through a
careful, informed craftsperson. This
person works only for his Lord. The
message rests solely in the Gospel.

2 Tim. 2:22-26
The two pests described here should
make sense to teenagers. The
temptations of youth are very real to
them. Rather than pointing out the
evils of the sins described, point out
the effect that such living has on
congregational life. The same can be
said for quarrels. Teenagers know how
miserable quarrels make them feel.

Emphasize, therefore, how sinful pride usually is the basis for them.

Paul's description of noble and ignoble articles refers to utensils used for partying compared with those used for noble purposes. We certainly would want to wash articles used for partying before we would use them for other purposes. Emphasize that God cleans us through Baptism. The quote from Luther should recall the daily purpose of our Baptism.

2 Tim. 3:1—4:5

The enemy now takes on human form. The first can be seen on any TV. This is the typical TV preacher who gathers in millions to build his or her own empire at the expense of God's kingdom. Be careful about designating actual personalities, for we cannot look into hearts. But we can see results and emphases.

The companion to the TV preacher is the preacher who has only "good" news—not the Good News of Christ, but the sweet promises of success. Note that Scripture also contains the news of humanity's sinfulness and the need to depend totally on God's grace.

Perhaps that is why Paul again reminds Timothy of the Scripture's origin and its purpose. When it trusts God as its Author and seeks the purposes listed, each congregation has all the power and the only message it needs.

PRACTICE (Objectives 3—4)

1. If possible, do the suggested roleplaying activities. Refer to session 5 for a review of roleplaying suggestions. As students roleplay today, do not let the demonstration of negative results overshadow the positive demonstration of God's solutions.

Expect laughter and enjoyment during this activity. Don't be surprised at how observant students are of adult behavior. Above all, keep the emphasis on God's positive solutions.

2. As the need arises, adjust the questions to be answered in the report. The final four questions will be presented in session 19.

WRAP—UP

After a rather loose roleplaying activity, individual silent prayers for individual congregations would be in order.

Session 19: Measuring Success

BIBLE BASIS: 2 Tim. 4:6—8, 14—18

CENTRAL TRUTH

God does not measure a congregation's success in terms of large buildings or financial surpluses. Rather, God uses a measuring stick of how faithfully a congregation proclaims the Gospel and how firmly it holds on to its hope of an eternal inheritance.

OBJECTIVES

That the students will

1. identify the true signs of congregational success as being centered in Christ's victory for them;

2. identify a congregation's main goals as receiving the crown of righteousness and proclaiming the good news of salvation;

3. describe worldly measures of congregational success;

4. establish priorities for congregational activities on the basis of Scriptural principles;

5. describe important programs in their congregations.

BACKGROUND

During this session you may be tempted to dwell on the negative aspects of outward signs of congregational success. Resist temptations to put down God's gifts to congregations of financial success, members, programs, and outward growth. We should view these as gifts from the Lord. At the same time we should recognize the dangers of becoming more concerned with them than with the church's most important goals. Highlight those goals during this session.

Pray that the Holy Spirit will work in the hearts of your students a burning desire to receive eternal salvation and to proclaim the Gospel.

STRETCHING

As we approach another session of concluding activities, we again use "Stretching" to help students review. This activity asks the students to recall the analogy of a congregation to plant growth.

The answers could read as follows:
1. The Word of God
2. God, through His spokespersons
3. The world of hearers
4. The work of the Holy Spirit
5. **The miracle of conversion**
6. Satan's efforts to stamp out the church
7. The evidences of the Holy Spirit's work (the fruit of faith)
8. The efforts of a congregation to proclaim the Word
9. The final gathering of the church into glory

GETTING THE WORD   (Objectives 1–2)

Verses 6–8

1. Paul expressed his accomplishments in the past tense, indicating that he knew that his death was near. He had fought the good fight, finished the race, and kept the faith.

2. Paul (and we) receive the crown of righteousness as a gift. It is God's righteousness, given to those who believe (Rom. 3:21–28).

3–4. All three are the work of the Holy Spirit, who kept Paul in the faith (Jude 24).

5. The world cannot see this, and therefore praise and glory are not forthcoming from it. A person's salvation is a private matter, accomplished solely through God's efforts and rejoiced over in heaven and by those of a like spirit here on earth.

Verses 14–18

1. Alexander the metal worker tried to hinder Paul's message.

2. God gave Paul His strength so Paul could proclaim His message.

3. Paul gave God credit for this success of proclaiming the Gospel of Jesus Christ.

4. Summing up, the two goals of a congregation are receiving the crown of righteousness (salvation) and proclaiming the Gospel.

Do not proceed until students clearly understand these two goals. All others marks of a congregation's success must be measured by these two.

PRACTICE   (Objectives 3––5)

1. Actually the two goals are one. Those who receive the crown of righteousness do proclaim the Gospel. You cannot have one without the other. **("Faith without deeds is dead" [James 2:26].)**

Each item listed could either help or hinder the attainment of the primary success marks. For example:

Large membership helps in that more people may hear the Gospel. It hinders if it leads to efforts only to gain members.

Beautiful buildings help if they set the mood for meaningful worship, for hearing the Word. They hinder if they lead to pride in buildings or if a congregation expends too much effort to maintain them.

A well-known, gifted preacher helps by proclaiming the Word powerfully. He hinders if he tries to gain fame as a personality. A full calendar helps if each activity becomes an opportunity to proclaim the Word. It hinders if people are busy for busy's sake, just to looks good.

A large budget helps in that it provides resources to spread the Gospel. It hinders if money is used to make the church look prosperous.

Friendly people help if they use their friendliness to share their faith. This hinders if friendliness becomes a major goal in and of itself.

Music can become an opportunity to express our faith, to proclaim the Gospel. It hinders when the music, not the Gospel, becomes the goal when we seek fame for ourselves.

Active youth groups give a great opportunity to share the Word. They hinder if they become social clubs and when the goal becomes large membership.

2. Try to get students to list some claims to fame of local congregations. Discuss their pluses and minuses.

3. If possible, do this in small groups. Lively discussion should

result. Respect all opinions. Use this activity as a gauge of the class's grasp of the congregation's prime goal.

You might expand this by making a list appropriate to your school. It, too, is a congregation of sorts.

4. This is the final set of questions. Clarify final instructions, format requirements, and deadlines.

WRAP-UP

Conclude with prayers for individual congregations represented in your class. Include needs, strengths, and ministries brought to light during discussions.

Session 20: Concluding Activities for Units 3-4

Reread the comments on reviews found in Session 10.

The review for units 3-4 takes the format of short answers. You might add review questions for vocabulary, concepts, and relationships.

The first 18 questions closely follow materials that students have worked with in units 3-4. Questions 19 and 20 are opinion questions that require students to make judgments based on their understandings of these two units.

1. Why should God be worshiped ahead of anything or anyone else?

(God has created us, redeemed us, and keeps us in the faith. Our spiritual and physical being belong to Him.)

2. Give one example (not in a church service) of how a "called-out one" worships God.

(A "called-out one" worships God when he or she does anything for God's glory.)

3. What are the differences between private and corporate worship?

(Private worship has no set form. No set order is needed for a personal relationship with God. Corporate worship always involves others. Therefore it requires a unity of purpose and action.)

4. Why does Paul say that worship should be orderly?

(Paul says that worship should be orderly because God is a God of peace.)

5. Explain sacramental and sacrificial acts of worship.

(Sacramental acts are acts in which God gives His grace to the church. Sacrificial acts are those in which the church reacts to God's grace and gives Him love and devotion.)

6. Give two examples each of sacramental and sacrifical worship. Explain what happens in each and tell why.

(Sacramental: Reading the Word; God gives us instruction, and the Gospel. The sacraments; God gives us forgiveness through Word and physical elements.

Sacrificial: Songs [we praise God using music]. Prayers [we talk to God in a unified way]. Both are reactions to His grace.)

7. Describe liturgical worship.

(Liturgical worship has a long history, has changed through the years, contains a balance of sacramental and sacrificial elements, has a set framework to help us worship God together, and allows variation from week to week.)

8. What are three criteria for any gift we bring to the Lord?

(A result of grace; voluntary; a gift to God or others [Col. 3:15-16])

9. What does "edify" mean? How does Paul apply it to corporate worship?

(Edify means to build up another's faith. Paul says that nothing should be done unless it can edify the worshipers.)

10. For what reason do worshipers stand, sit, and kneel in a service?

(Worshipers stand to praise, pray, and to show respect. They sit to be instructed. They kneel for confession and during some prayers.)

11. What three things need to exist to have a Christian congregation?

(Someone needs to speak the Gospel, there must be hearers, and the Holy Spirit must be present.)

12. How is a congregation like a plant?

(A congregation starts from seed, the Word; is germinated by the power of the Holy Spirit; is nurtured by the water of God's Word; is tended by God's ministers; and exists to grow and to spread the seed of the Word to other places.)

13. What mandate does God give to pastors and congregations?

(To make disciples of all nations, by preaching and baptizing.)

14. Which of the following comes closest to a congregation: a country club, a corporation, a government, or a school? Why?

(Probably a school, because a congregation teaches the Gospel to itself and to others.)

15. Name and describe three enemies of the congregation.

(Those who argue over word meanings; those who tempt young members with sinful desires; those who preach only for their own welfare.)

16. What does Paul say is God's all-purpose weapon against these enemies? Give two examples of how it can be used.

(The Word. Against those who distort the Word, a careful workman can use the Gospel to show how Christ is the answer to all needs. Against youthful

temptations, Paul refers to a daily washing in baptism. We can use it daily.)

17. What are the two goals of a successful congregation?

(For all its members to receive the crown of righteousness [salvation] and to proclaim the Gospel.)

18. What are the signs that these goals have been reached?

(Only in heaven will we see the first. Evidence of the second appears when the congregation proclaims the entire Word of God in word and deed at all times.)

19. Write what you would tell a person who did not attend corporate worship because the pastor did not preach good sermons.

(Answers will vary.)

20. Write what the first two major tasks would be if you were a missionary beginning a new congregation. Give reasons for your choices.

(Answers will vary.)

Permission is herewith granted to duplicate the above questions for testing or review. Please add the following credit line: Concordia Publishing House copyright 1987. Used by permission.

Unit 5: Witnessing, the Church's Work

This is by far the largest unit and comprises a major thrust of the course. Far from being a means of earning God's favor, witnessing is seen as the evidence of God's Spirit at work in the church.

Witnessing is the outside work of the church. In order to make this task a personal matter, we will follow the career of St. Paul in this unit.

Through him we will see how God calls each individual, each congregation, and indeed the entire church to witness for Him.

In addition to witnessing by speaking, in this unit we try to help students recognize that they can witness in other ways. When we live the Christian life, we present a powerful witness to the world.

Session 21: Getting Started

BIBLE BASIS: Acts 1:8; 9:19b–29; Gal. 1:11–24

CENTRAL TRUTH

The Holy Spirit chooses His witnesses to speak and live the Gospel wherever they are. St. Paul is an example of such a witness.

OBJECTIVES

That the students will

1. identify people of many occupations who were witnesses for the Lord;

2. describe Christ's plan for reaching the world with the Gospel;

3. describe the urgency with which

St. Paul began his ministry;

   4. tell about the power of the Holy Spirit in redirecting lives;

   5. experience being witnesses.

BACKGROUND

Notice the change in organization in the Student Book for this session. The titles liken the session activities to an athletic contest with a "Warm—up," "First Half," and "Second Half."

Take a few minutes to think about the miracle reported in Acts 9. How could someone be "breathing out murderous threats against the Lord's disciples" (v. 1), and a short time later "preach in the synogogues that Jesus is the Son of God" (v. 20)? Marvel again at the power of the Holy Spirit as we see it revealed in this chapter.

Think about the way the Holy Spirit has changed lives of people you know. How has He moved some of them to witness? Think of personal experiences you can share to demonstrate that the Holy Spirit is indeed alive and well today.

Pray that as you teach this session the Holy Spirit will work through God's Word to awaken in your students a renewal to witnessing for your Lord and Savior.

WARM—UP   (Objective 1)

The occupation of these Bible authors supported the work of witnessing. Following are possible answers:

   1. Luke
   2. Nehemiah
   3. Solomon or David
   4. Ezra or Ezekiel
   5. Paul
   6. Daniel or Nehemiah
   7. Moses or David
   8. Matthew
   9. Peter or John
   10. Joshua

FIRST HALF   (Objectives 2—4)

Acts 1:8

Make sure students understand the three parts of this verse, as explained. The importance of the term *witness* will be discussed and practiced in "Second Half." The summary (4) should read:

   a. The Holy Spirit
   b. Witness
   c. Home, to surrounding areas, to the world

Acts 9:19b—29

Review, if necessary, the events of Saul's conversion (Acts 9:1—19a). Do this only for background. Use this section to show the effect of the Holy Spirit on Saul and how he began his witness. The answers to the questions could read as follows:

   1. Saul began "at once" (v. 20), a ministry marked by "speaking boldly" (v. 28). Saul did not sit around and wait for the right time.

   2. In Damascus Saul baffled the Jews, who tried to kill him. In Jerusalem he talked and debated with the Grecian Jews, who also tried to kill him.

   3. When Saul tried to join the disciples, they did not believe he was a disciple. Saul must have also been discouraged when he was ushered out of Palestine back home to Tarsus.

   4. He continued speaking boldly and moved about freely in the name of the Lord.

   5. The "brothers" probably feared for Saul's life. It's also possible that his strong witness made their ministry more difficult.

   6. Saul moved in the power of the Spirit, he boldly witnessed the name of Christ, and he did this where he was at the time (Damascus and Jerusalem).

Gal. 1:11—24

   1. Paul stresses that his Gospel came from the Lord and not from someone else (verses 11—12, 16—17, and 18—20).

   2. Luke stresses Saul's urgency in speaking for Christ, almost to the point of fanaticism. Even though his life was endangered, he continued.

   3. The Acts and Galatians accounts are similar in that they show the power of the Spirit in teaching and empowering Saul to be a strong witness.

   4. It seems that Paul's information came from his studies as a Pharisee and from the Lord Himself (Gal. 1:12, 14, and 17).

SECOND HALF (Objectives 4–5)

1. Following are the people who were filled with the Holy Spirit, along with their actions:
a. 70 elders of Israel prophesied
b. Samson tore a lion apart
c. Saul prophesied
d. Ezekiel ate a scroll
e. Zechariah prophesied
f. Apostles spoke in new tongues

2. Have a volunteer or two read the quote as they wrote it. Or divide the class into pairs and have each person insert his or her partner's name into the reading.

3. **Plan to use this activity.** Through it demonstrate the role of a witness. You, as the judge or lawyer, should use a very formal manner to ask questions of various students. Begin by asking them easy questions about themselves and their activities. Gradually shift the questions to the subject of their beliefs. A sample is provided. The outcome should be obvious: to be a witness one needs only to speak about things that he or she knows.

a. What is your name?
b. What is your address?
c. What is your locker number?
d. At this moment, what is on the top shelf of your locker?
e. What would you do if those items were stolen?
f. How do you feel about thieves?
g. How do you think God feels about thieves?
h. What did Jesus once say to a thief?
i. Why did He say this?

Develop any track, using humor also, but eventually steer the questioning around to something that Jesus said or did. Match the questions to the personality of the student.

FINAL WHISTLE

Conclude with a reading of the Great Commission (**Matt. 28:18–20**) and the Great Doxology of **Jude 24–25.**

Session 22: Witnessing Where You Are

BIBLE BASIS: John 4:4–26

CENTRAL TRUTH

God gives His "called-out ones" the opportunity and the power to witness wherever we are. These opportunities may be to speak for Christ to the unbeliever as well as to fellow "called-out ones."

OBJECTIVES

That the students will
1. relate that we usually witness away from church;
2. tell how Jesus witnessed;
3. demonstrate the ability to speak to others about Christ;
4. describe the many opportunities for witnessing that exist each day.

BACKGROUND

We could call this session "Jesus' Manual on Being Fishers of Men." Based on **John 4** (The Woman at the Well), this session will emphasize how easy and how natural it can be to include the Gospel as a part of our conversations.

"Second Half" suggests that students practice some evangelism techniques. Before they begin, you may want to provide more detail about one evangelism strategy. Get information from the evangelism committee of a local congregation. Write for information on dialog evangelism or Teacher Witness Workshops from Board for Evangelism Services, The Lutheran Church—Missouri Synod, 1333 South Kirkwood Road, Saint Louis, MO 63122-7295. Also examine the suggestions in session 15 of *For God So Loved . . . .,* a 9th-grade course in the Lutheran High School Religion Series.

Pray that the Holy Spirit will work through the words from John's gospel to motivate and empower your students to witness where they are.

WARM-UP (Objective 1)

To get started, spring this word-association game on the class. The activity will show how we associate certain activities with certain places or situations. Read the list quickly in this order.

1. family   5. tent
2. study   6. June
3. gymnasium   7. office
4. hamburger   8. Bible

The word associations should show that we tend to equate Bible with church and school or with some formal use. During this session students should see how God's Word can be used at any time and in any place (Deut. 6:6–9).

FIRST HALF (Objectives 1–2)

The text, **John 4:4–26**, contains several Gospel lessons. You may want to get into one or two of them (check a commentary for suggestions), but save enough time to get into the focus of **the Student Book material**: the technique Jesus used to prepare the woman for a meaningful proclamation of the Gospel.

The Bait (verses 4–15)

1. Jesus used water for "bait." Water was a precious commodity in Palestine.

2. The woman certainly would be interested in anything that would relieve her of her chore of carrying water.

3. Jesus proclaimed that His water would **"become in him a spring . . . to eternal life"** (v. 14). This was His first solid reference to the spiritual. **"Living water"** (v. 10) aroused her curiosity.

4. In **v. 15** she told Jesus, **"Sir, give me this water."**

5. Jesus was offering the "water" of Good News of salvation through Him. Note that this was pure Gospel.

The Hook (verses 16–20)

1. The woman was a prostitute. Maybe she was drawing water at noon to attempt to avoid the snide remarks of the town ladies.

2. Jesus revealed—and the woman noticed—that He knew more than was normal (**"Sir, I can see that You are a prophet"**—v. 19)!

3. We like to change the subject when someone gets too close to our sins, and that is what the woman did. People do not like to see how God's law makes them look.

The Line and Pole (verses 21–26)

1. Jesus pointed out that the only prerequisites for worship (whether Jew or Samaritan) were **"spirit and truth"** (vv. 23–24). Both are signs of a "called-out one."

2. The woman mentioned the Messiah (**v. 25**). He who would straighten out the conflict between Jews and Samaritans. This may have been her way of putting off her own moral problems.

3. Jesus said, **"I who speak to you am He"** (v. 26). He gave a forthright presentation of the Gospel.

4. The woman's request to the townspeople and their reply show the beginning of faith. They responded, **"This man really is the Savior of the world"** (v. 42).

SECOND HALF (Objectives 3–4)

1. Students should do this activity outside of class. Have them share results in groups or, better yet, with the entire class. They should find hundreds of opportunities to speak for Christ in a natural, everyday setting. These results are to be used as the warm-up for *session 23*.

2. If most of your class have studied *For God So Loved . . . .*, take time to review the activity in the second column of page 34. If they have not studied this, present it or another formal evangelism technique before you begin the roleplay.

The roleplaying activity will provide an opportunity to try out Jesus' technique. Be selective in choosing participants. As a matter of fact, you might be the witness in the first roleplay. "Choose for success"; insure that the first demonstrations are good examples.

The five-minute time limit has been suggested to emphasize that we need to take the initiative to present a Christian witness; we need to avoid exchanging only pleasantries and nothings. Note that this technique for witnessing does not require an answer to the Gospel presentation. If one comes, thank God. But "getting a commitment" is not a part of the technique. The commitment comes through the work of the Holy Spirit and not as a result of our efforts.

You might wish to extend this **activity through the week.**

FINAL WHISTLE
Say, **When an evangelism team calls** on **unchurched persons, they often end their meeting with prayer.** In your prayer today thank the Lord for the many Christian witnesses given during this class period.

Session 23: Speaking to the Neighborhood

BIBLE BASIS: Acts 11:19-30

CENTRAL TRUTH
The Holy Spirit moves "called-out ones" to be witnesses in their communities, individually and collectively, and He blesses those efforts.

OBJECTIVES
That the students will
1. identify people who need to hear the Gospel of Jesus Christ;
2. describe the role of the congregation in being a witness to the community;
3. recall examples of how God's people have witnessed to their Lord wherever they were.

BACKGROUND
This session reinforces the session 22 concept of "witnessing where you are." This session, however, emphasizes the collective witness of a congregation. To reinforce this concept, much of this session is to be done in discussion groups. Plan to move to individual study, though, for "Second Half."
As you examine the miracles that occurred in the Acts incident, emphasize especially the power of the Holy Spirit as discussed in the last two questions of **"First Half."** We sow, but He provides the increase. The same promise applies to you personally as you present God's Word to those in your class.
Pray that God will empower your students to build one another up, thus encouraging them to witness individually and collectively.

WARM-UP (Objective 1)
Reactivate discussion groups as a means of making use of the surveys of session 22. Encourage the students to name names and to be forthright as they share information. Allow adequate time for this, but do not allow conversation to wander.
As groups discuss question 3, encourage them to get beyond, "To tell them that Jesus died for them." This is certainly true, but we need to shape this marvelous news into practical everyday expressions. Perhaps we can begin with the glorious message of Rom. 8:32: **"He who did not spare His own Son, but gave Him up for us all—how will He not also, along with Him, graciously give us all things?"** "All things" certainly includes freedom from worry, assurance of divine guidance, etc.

FIRST HALF (Objective 2)
Do not impose your answers on a group, but bring a group back on track if they wander. Following are some possible conclusions based on the reading.

Verses 19-21
1. An evangelism group takes the Gospel beyond the members (Jews) and contacts the outsiders (Gentiles).
2. Their only message was **"the good news about the Lord Jesus"** (v. 20). Some congregations today emphasize the same message, but others seem more concerned with gaining members, pledging for a walk-a-thon, selling tickets to suppers, etc.

Verses 22-24
1. His main role was that of encouragement. (Barnabas means "son of encouragement.") Also by his example he demonstrated the power of the Spirit. Mainly, however, he was able to see beyond noses, and recognize God's grace at work among souls.
2. The example of Barnabas suggests that a pastor should build up the "called-out ones." *They* are the main contact of Christ with the community.

Of course, as they have opportunity, pastors should also witness to the community.

Verses 25-26

1. Among the activities were many Bible classes (v. 26), individual counseling sessions (v. 26), and gathering and distributing gifts for the poor (vv. 29-30).

2. Perhaps the name "Christian" at first was a put down, coined by enemies of Christ. But, as with the cross (a symbol of shame), the followers of Christ wore it proudly.

Verses 27-30

1. By gathering the gifts of God's people, a congregation can help care for the poor, homeless, sick, and starving.

2. Allow discussion to flow on this one. Direct them to Gal. 6:10 as a key guideline: "Do good to all people, especially to those who belong to the family of believers."

3. Strongly emphasize the message of these verses: When people believe in the Lord Jesus Christ, it is the "Lord's hand" (v. 21) that "brings" them. Monetary gifts are but one evidence of faith at work.

4. As the Lord does the converting, the church can confidently continue its witness, knowing God's Word "will not return . . . empty" (Is. 55:11). At the same time, the church should realize that the only means for dispensing the word is--the church.

SECOND HALF (Objective 3)

This activity reinforces "Witnessing Where You Are." Following are the references and names:
1. **Acts 8:26-40;** Philip
2. **1 Sam. 16:23;** David
3. **Gen. 40:6-8;** Joseph
4. **2 Kings 5:2;** Young girl
5. **Acts 16:22-34;** Paul and Silas
6. **Judg. 6:24-32;** Gideon
7. **Acts 10:23-48;** Peter
8. **Genesis 12:4-9;** Abram
9. **Acts 18:1-3;** Paul, Aquila, and Priscilla
10. **Num. 14:1-9;** Caleb and Joshua

FINAL WHISTLE

If the period ends while the groups are intact, the leader of each group could add a sentence to the prayer on behalf of individuals or congregations that were mentioned in discussion. If individual work is being done, select individuals to be the prayer leaders.

Session 24: Speaking to the World (Part 1)

BIBLE BASIS: Acts 19:1-41

CENTRAL TRUTH

Jesus calls and empowers His "called-out ones" to be His witnesses to the entire world. Paul's experiences in Ephesus show the effects of the Gospel in the world.

OBJECTIVES

That the students will

1. compare incidents from Paul's ministry in Ephesus with the effect of the Word in the world today;

2. describe problems God and His church need to overcome as we bring His Word to various areas of the world today;

3. relate one purpose of a synod or association: to bring the Gospel to the world;

4. describe the progress of the

Gospel throughout the world.

BACKGROUND

Sessions 24-25 will examine the church's mission to the world. In session 24 we compare Ephesus to the world. You might wish to read additional background material on Ephesus as a means of relating it to our world today. This comparison should show how, even at this late date, the world still is the same spiritually and still needs the same Gospel.

This guide provides sketchy information about the spread of the Gospel throughout the world. To expand on this information with your class, read about the spread of Christianity in an encyclopedia or a church-history book.

Pray that God will bless your

presentation of this lesson and will move your students to speak to the world personally and through support of others.

WARM-UP (Objective 1)

You will need to make many of the points of comparison between Ephesus and the world today as this section is read. For example:

1. Both consider economic success the prime goal. Think of the importance of trade balances, tariffs, foreign investments, etc.

2. Both are concerned over any loss to their economy.

3. Both worship at the feet of pleasure, whether called Artemis (Diana) or Mass Media. Both find pleasure in exploitation of sex and in the buying and selling of substances that produce pleasure.

4. The Gospel of Christ gives to humanity the peaceful relationship with God, while the temptation of Satan continues to be: **"All this [the world] I will give you if you will bow down and worship me"** (Matt. 4:9).

FIRST HALF (Objectives 1 and 2)

After discussing these similarities, have the students read the sections indicated. The evidences of Satan's handiwork should be obvious: the Jews' rejection of the Gospel, demon possession, the occult and sorcery, idolatry, the desire for economic security, riot and disorder. You might complete these sentences as a class project.

Verses 1-22

Possible answers:

1. Rented the Hall of Tyrannus where he proclaimed the Gospel for two years, and many therefore heard the Word.

2. Handkerchiefs and aprons that were taken to the sick, who were healed and freed of evil spirits.

3. Many evil spirits were driven out, people openly confessed their sins, books and scrolls about sorcery were burned.

4. 20.

Verses 23-41

1. They were losing money when people gave up idolatry and believed in Christ, therefore not buying idol-related objects.

2. He was the one through whom the Gospel had been proclaimed, and his life was in danger.

3. They (the Christians) had not robbed temples or blasphemed Artemis.

4. The people were in danger of creating a riot and could not justify such commotion to the authorities.

Ephesus and the World Today

Answers in this section could vary widely. Accept any that seem reasonable. Following are examples:

1. *Europe*: The Gospel is now almost lost in state religions and tradition.

2. *Africa and Asia*: The Gospel will have greater impact if it includes deeds as well as words, if it addresses problems brought on by disease and starvation.

3. *New Guinea*: Many tribes have only recently heard the Gospel. Some superstition may still exist.

4. *Communist countries*: Leaders consider religion a human defect that hinders attempts to create wealth.

5. *The United States*: Wealth and pleasure abound and seem to rule out any need for God--much less a Savior from sin.

SECOND HALF (Objective 3)

Use whatever material or illustrations you have to make clear the purpose of a synod or association. Dispel the notion that they are "superchurches" that hand out regulations for all to follow. Stress the voluntary cooperation aspect.

1. Assign reports for completion as soon as possible. The school library should have some material on this subject.

2. You might draw arrows on the map to show the following events, together with the time when they occurred:
--Christ issues the Great Commission: *A. D. 29*
--The Apostles to the Roman Empire: *A.D. 40-100*
--Paul to Greece and Rome: *A. D. 45-63*
--To Europe: *A. D. 300-1400*
--Post Reformation Mission Thrusts to North America, South America, and India: *A. D. 1500-1600*

--North American Missions to Asia:
   Early 1900s
--North American Missions to Africa:
   Middle 1900s to Present
--North American Missions to New
   Guinea: *Late 1900s to Present*

   Add other information your students
suggests or that you found through your

research of church history.

WRAP-UP
   Have one student read Matt. 24:9-14.
Then have other students read Rev.
22:12-17 and Rev. 22:18-20. Ask
everyone to join together in saying
verse 21.

Session 25: Speaking to the World (Part 2)

BIBLE BASIS: Acts 2:1-21; 2 Cor.
11:21b-33; Phil. 3:7-9

CENTRAL TRUTH
   God calls certain individuals to be
missionaries to the world and works
mightily in their lives to help them
accomplish that task. He fills them
with love for the Lord Jesus Christ,
thus motivating them to go and work for
Him.

OBJECTIVES
   That the students will
   1. explain that Christ calls people
to do mission work;
   2. describe the personal sacrifices
that missionaries give to their Lord;
   3. identify love for Christ as the
underlying motivation for all true
mission work;
   4. express a desire to correspond
with a missionary.

BACKGROUND
   As the culmination to the topic of
witnessing, the students are asked to
write letters to current missionaries.
An annual *Directory of Missionary
Personnel* provides a list of
missionaries serving missions of The
Lutheran Church--Missouri Synod. Each
pastor of the LCMS receives a copy of
this directory. If you cannot secure
one locally, ask for one from Board for
Mission Services, The Lutheran Church--
Missouri Synod, 1333 South Kirkwood
Road, St. Louis, MO 63122-7295.
Check with your District office to
receive names of local missionaries.
   You might also want to tell students
about various types of ministries to
foreign countries, such as Bible
translators, evangelistic missionaries,
educational missionaries, health
workers, literacy workers, business

managers, construction supervisors, and
volunteer youth ministers. Write to
the same address for information about
these ministries.
   Pray that the Holy Spirit will fill
your students with love for those who
carry out special mission work, and
that He will move each of your students
to encourage at least one of them.

WARM-UP (Objective 1)
   Refer to the map in session 24 and
the various mission thrusts mentioned.
Be sure your students understand that
missions happens only when people share
God's Word. During this session
students can get acquainted with such
people.

FIRST HALF (Objectives 2-3)
   A resume for St. Paul might include
the following facts:
   1. Born in Tarsus in Cilicia.
   2. Taught by Gamaliel, chief among
highly respected rabbis of Jerusalem
   3. Converted in Damascus
   4. Baptized by Ananias
   5. Changed name from Saul (Hebrew)
to Paul (Gentile)
   6. Endured 5 beatings with whips; 3
beatings with rods; 1 stoning; 3
shipwrecks; a day and a night in the
sea; constant moving; dangers from
rivers, from bandits, from Jews, from
Gentiles, in cities, in the country, at
sea, from false brothers; lack of food,
sleep, and clothing; pressure of
concern for the congregations
   7. Escaped from Damascus in a basket
   8. Suffered **a thorn in my flesh**
(2 Cor. 12:7)
   9. Realized that God's strength is
seen when he is weak
   10. Asked Timothy to bring his cloak,
scrolls, and parchments
   11. Answers will vary.

SECOND HALF (Objective 4)

To keep this from being just another school exercise, sense the pulse of your students and adjust as needed. Encourage them to make personal contact with those who witness on their behalf. The best approach would be to make this an optional activity. For those who genuinely want to correspond, provide the information suggested. Also provide information on postage and postal regulations. Use your best judgment as to whether to read or edit the letters.

For those not so motivated, assign a short report on a missionary from the past. Prepare a list from a church history book.

WRAP-UP

End with silent prayers for individual missionaries. Encourage students to include one missionary per day on their prayer lists, at least for a week or so.

Session 26: Witnessing by Imitation

BIBLE BASIS: 2 Cor. 2:14—3:2; Eph. 4:1-16

CENTRAL TRUTH

God calls and empowers "called-out ones" to witness not only with words, but also with deeds, as we imitate God's love in our lives. God uses those deeds to strengthen the power of our words.

OBJECTIVES

That the students will

1. explain that being an imitator of God is a way of demonstrating our love for Him;

2. tell how the church imitates God when it is unified and does Jesus' work in a mature manner;

3. demonstrate their understanding of imitating God by relating it to witnessing in daily life.

BACKGROUND

When we speak about Christ, it's very obvious that we are witnessing to those around us. Unfortunately many Christians excuse themselves from this aspect by claiming they can't speak.

The next six sessions will focus on the fact that witnessing can also be done by example. As you teach, help your students avoid the pitfall of concentrating on mere morality: "be a better person." Emphasize that Christ was perfect for us, that His power empowers us, and that through our imitating we are merely expressing our love to Him.

Pray that the Holy Spirit will move your students to want to do works of service, and that, as they do these works, they keep before them the goal of building up the body of Christ.

WARM-UP (Objectives 1-2)

The one-word theme for this session is *imitation*, based on **Eph. 5:1.** Spend some time on a free exchange on how much of life is based on imitation. Put a list of examples on the board, making as large a display as possible to demonstrate the point.

Make the transition to the fact that a Christian's entire life is one of imitating God. Stress that we strive to imitate God's attribute of love. You might wish to add that Satan tries to get us to imitate the other attributes of God: omniscience, omnipotence, ownership of all things, etc., but not love.

FIRST HALF (Objective 2)

Imitation One: Unity (Eph. 4:1-6)

1. Following are examples of the oneness God has given us:

   One body--the church
   One Spirit--the Holy Spirit
   One hope--eternal life with God
   One Lord--Jesus Christ
   One faith--in Jesus Christ as our
      Savior
   One baptism--water and the Word
   One God--the triune God,
      Creator of all.

2. These marks of unity must have made quite an impressions on the Ephesian readers, because of the wide differences in backgrounds that existed there. No matter of what time, place,

background, or race, the church is unified in:

a. *Belief*--in Jesus Christ as Savior
b. *Means of grace*--Word and Sacrament
c. *Destination*--an eternity with God
d. *Work*--witnessing to each other and to the world

Imitation Two: Work (Eph. 4:7-12a)

In the prologue to this section (vv. 7-10), Paul quotes Ps. 68:18. The eternally divine Christ, the true God who fills the entire universe, is in the perfect position to give to the church the gifts listed.

1. God gave the church apostles, prophets, evangelists, pastors, and teachers to "prepare God's people for works of service" (v. 12a).

2. The gifts of the Spirit mentioned here are those that communicate the Word of God to people. Since no one in the church today has been an eyewitness to Christ's resurrection, the gift of apostle does not appear to exist today (Acts 1:21-22). Leaders in the church do, however, continue to imitate the work God gave to the early church through prophets, evangelists, pastors, and teachers.

Perhaps many of your students cannot see themselves ever taking on one of the above roles. Help them focus on the **"works of service"** (Eph. 4:12a) they can perform for the other members of the church.

Imitation Three: Maturity (Eph. 4:12b-16)

1. **Verse 12b** offers many opportunities for variation. Remind the students to check back to session 5 for ideas.

2. In 1 Cor. 3:1-4 Paul referred to the Corinthians as **"mere infants"**

because of their lack of spiritual depth (*mere babies in the faith*). Their behavior apparently was more worldly than Christ-like.

3. Answers for these references are as follows:

1 Sam. 20:24-33: Jonathan stuck up for David to his father Saul, who was bent on killing David.

Mark 8:31-33: Jesus addressed Peter as **Satan** when Peter objected to Jesus' going to Jerusalem to suffer and die.

Acts 15:1-2: Paul and Barnabas disagreed sharply with Jewish Christians who taught that salvation also depended on keeping the laws of Moses.

Acts 21:10-14: Agabus and other friends of Paul tried to get him to change his mind about going to Jerusalem.

4. Eph. 4:16 summarizes the 3 imitations as follows:

Unity: **"The whole body, joined and held together"**

Work: **"as each part does its work."**

Maturity: **"grows and builds itself up in love."**

SECOND HALF (Objective 3)

Follow the directions in the Student Book. Make every effort to have the students write in the *third person*, to avoid the danger of a *self-testimonial*. You will use these stories during "Second Half" in session 28, so assign them to be finished by then. Add more titles as idea starters.

FINAL WHISTLE

Conclude with prayers for those who communicate God's Word to people in the church today.

Session 27: Imitating at Home

BIBLE BASIS: Eph. 5:22—6:4

CENTRAL TRUTH

The analogy of Christ and the church illustrates the relationship God desires between husbands and wives. Christ loves the church and through that love provides the basis for husbands and wives to love each other

and for parents and children to do the same. In this way a proper family is truly like the church.

OBJECTIVES

That the students will

1. tell how members of a family witness to each other;

2. identify Christ as the husband

and the church as His bride in the analogy Paul presents;

3. **tell how the bond between husband and wife is built on love, not on domination and submission;**

4. demonstrate that they understand this analogy.

BACKGROUND

The format of this session differs from that of previous sessions. In addition to a careful reading of the text **(Eph. 5:22—6:4),** the students are to read a detailed explanation of this famous analogy by St. Paul. Because the analogy is so unique, its treatment here is unique also.

One might ask, "How does the subject of husband and wife relationships relate to the subject of witnessing?" If the church is to be a strong witness by doing, it must begin at home with husband, wife, parents, and children. When marriage is built on the foundation blocks of Christ's love for the church and the church's love for Christ, that family has a firm footing from which to reach out to the unsaved.

In **Ephesians** this text falls within the greater context of the grace and peace we have from Christ and of the power we have to love *because He loves us.* **Be sure that students do not lose sight of the Gospel during this session.** All of us, when we look at the measuring stick God gives us here, fall far short. None of us can love as Christ loved. Without the Gospel, we would despair. Pray that God will empower you to teach in a way that will build hope, not despair, in the hearts of your students.

Look ahead to session 29. Ask students to bring cassette tapes or other recordings of Christian music to play during class.

WARM—UP (Objective 1)

The procedure for this session is largely one of self study. Students should read the **"Warm—Up"** before reading either the text or the explanation.

FIRST HALF (Objectives 2-3)

Before getting into the readings, carefully discuss any student's concerns with striving for equality.

Probably some in your class will object to the phrase used by Paul, **"Wives, submit" (Eph. 5:22).** Assure them that this topic is the very one addressed in this reading.

SECOND HALF (Objective 4)

After students have read both the text and the Student Book explanations, provide them with copies of the questions reproduced here. Students should write their answers on their own paper. Correct them yourself or discuss them in class. Either way, be sure to allow class time to evaluate their answers.

Questions: Session 27—Imitating at Home

1. What analogy does Paul use to describe the marriage relationship?

2. Retell the story of Christ rescuing His bride: dying, rising again, and then marrying her. Use the frame of reference of a Western, a 19th-century melodrama, or a toned-down soap opera.

3. Why is *who is in charge* not a concern in this relationship between "called-out" husband and wife?

4. Why is there no rivalry between the head and the rest of the body (5:23)?

5. When Paul tells wives to submit to their husbands, what does he mean?

6. In 5:25–27 list what Christ has to do to make the church presentable.

7. Explain how a person will show care for his or her own body.

8. How will a Christian husband show that he loves his wife as his own body?

9. What will Christian marriage partners do when they fall short of the example of Christ and the church?

10. Why should children obey their parents?

11. List five examples for the husband and five examples for the wife in which they imitate Christ and the church in daily life.

12. On the basis of this reading, what qualities would you look for in a marriage partner?

Feel free to duplicate the above questions. Please add the following credit line: Concordia Publishing House, copyright 1987. Used by permission.

WRAP-UP

No answers are provided in this session. You might wish to eliminate some questions and add others. As you also work through these questions, additional insights may occur.

Grading and review are optional, but some evaluation and reinforcement should occur.

FINAL WHISTLE

As a concluding devotional activity, ask the students to pray for their parents or guardians. In an age when so many homes are broken, and so many children live in one-parent homes, more prayers need to be offered on their behalf.

Session 28: Before and After

BIBLE BASIS: Eph. 4:17-32

CENTRAL TRUTH

We are able to imitate God only because of the Holy Spirit's work, called sanctification. Through the power of the Spirit we are able to use the Ten Commandments as a basis for our imitation.

OBJECTIVES

That the students will

1. describe the activities of the unbelieving world;

2. identify God's work of conversion as the cause of the change that occurs in life-style when a person becomes a child of God;

3. demonstrate their understanding of how "called-out ones" use the Ten Commandments to show the new life within them;

4. share their experiences in observing the new life around them.

BACKGROUND

When the subject of doing good works comes up, we can very easily slip into the practice of moralizing, of failing to see in good works the work of the Holy Spirit.

Good works are merely the outward evidence of the Holy Spirit working inside the believer. Rather than patting ourselves on the back for being good, this session tries to *pat God on the back* for doing His good work of conversion and sanctification in us.

One activity in "Second Half" requires you to describe incidents in which you observed teenagers displaying positive actions. **Make notes for several days before class to prepare for this activity.** Another activity in "Second Half" requires students to read the stories they wrote for session 26.

As you prepare for this class, pray that the Holy Spirit will use you to lead His followers to display "after" behaviors.

WARM-UP

To highlight this introduction, cite a few examples of *before and after* articles from current magazines. The students can, no doubt, supply many of their own. Don't stay too long in the "Warm-Up," but make the transition into the real before-and-after story as found in Eph. 4:17-32.

FIRST HALF   (Objectives 1-2)

Eph. 4:17-19

1. Buzzwords have both an emotional and a cognitive impact. In these verses notice the negative emotional connotation of: futility; darkened; separated; ignorance; hardening; lost all sensitivity; sensuality; indulge; impurity; continual lust.

Take time to provide examples of this type of life-style. A current newspaper should provide more than enough examples. As you work through these examples, minimize the tendency to look at such behavior with amusement. You are looking at the signs of spiritual death. Looking at rotten vegetables and decaying meat doesn't cause laughter; just looking at spiritual death isn't funny either.

2. The two Biblical examples are presented in the same vein. This little-known story from Judges graphically illustrates what happens when separation from God takes over. Similarly, the story of Manasseh shows how rottenness can be started from the top. To further explain what Manasseh

did, you might want to read a commentary on this period of Israel's history.

Eph. 4:20-24

1. Students should copy vv. 23-24 as the description of this new life.

To illustrate this new creation of God, use the parable in **Matt. 22:1-14**. The party garment mentioned was always a part of a wealthy host's hospitality. Not wearing it, especially by a bum, would be the grossest of insults.

2. When God converts us, He covers us with the garment of His righteousness **(v. 24)**.

3. Not to wear God's righteousness means that we are satisfied with our own. Imagine telling God that **"our filthy rags"** (Is. 64:6) are better than the righteousness He provided at the cost of His own Son!

Eph. 4:25-32

These five actions of the new life are based on the Ten Commandments. The chart may be filled in this way:

1. a. 8. b. We are all one body and therefore do not withhold the truth from any part.

2. a. 5. b. Notice that of itself anger may not be a sin. But when anger is unjustified, especially if it grows into a feeling that lasts or a feeling of wanting to retaliate, it is sinful. The desired action is to express anger over a wrong action, not the doer.

3. a. 7. b. Do work for the benefit of those in need and not just for the benefit of self.

4. a. 8 or 2. b. Use talk to build up rather than to tear down. The finest type of helpful talk occurs when we use God's name to teach, praise, and pray.

5. a. 5. b. The finest expression of the new life is to forgive with no strings attached, just as God does for us.

If time allows, you might want to take up the negative aspect of the Ten Commandments; also stated in this section. They are: grieving the Holy Spirit; bitterness, rage and anger, brawling, and slander; malice. These were not included so that emphasis might be placed on the positive side of the Law.

SECOND HALF (Objectives 3-4)

1. For this activity you might need to take notes for a day or two to compile a list of examples. Your examples should be from what you observe around school. The students will probably use teachers as their examples. Make every effort to keep this positive. Even in this activity you and your students will be building up the body of Christ. The chart can be keep on the board.

2. By this time, the stories from session 26 should be done. Have students read them at this time.

FINAL WHISTLE

Read **Phil. 1:3-11** and allow time for silent prayers or meditation.

Session 29: Imitating the Light

BIBLE BASIS: Eph. 5:3-21

CENTRAL TRUTH

The Holy Spirit empowers us to live as children of the light. As such, we replace the immoral life of our sinful nature and of the sinful world around us with a life filled with the fruit of goodness, righteousness, and truth; with psalms, hymns, and spiritual songs.

OBJECTIVES

That the students will
1. recall the details of the witness of Paul and Silas to their Lord in Philippi;

2. identify present day parallels for the works of darkness and light on Paul's list;

3. tell how Jesus Christ brings light into dark lives with forgiveness and His new life;

4. express appreciation for the gift of Christian music, one of the finest examples of works of light.

BACKGROUND

In this session we continue with the theme of witnessing by imitating God.

Some Bibles, as a matter of fact, use one heading, "Living as Children of Light," for the entire section on which sessions 28-29 are based (Eph. 4:17—5:21). Since Ephesus was the center of the immoral cult of Diana, immorality abounded. This is perhaps why this section dwells so heavily on these sins.

Today we, too, live in an Ephesus-like culture that worships at the shrine of sex. We, too, can find plenty of real life opportunities to contrast these sins of darkness with the new life in Christ, a life of light. We have chosen to focus on music as we make this contrast. If something else would demonstrate the contrast more effectively for your class, adjust the lesson accordingly.

Before class select cassettes or records to use in class for **"Second Half."**

Pray again that the Holy Spirit will cause your students to imitate their Lord and Savior, especially this time by singing praises to Him.

WARM-UP (Objective 1)

Acts 16:16-40 reintroduces the life of Paul as a witness. Paul and Silas imitated God by casting out a demon, *suffering a beating even though innocent,* singing and praying in the presence of fellow prisoners, speaking the Gospel to the jailer and his household, and baptizing them.

Lead into the next section by stating that when the "going gets tough, the imitators of God get going."

FIRST HALF (Objectives 2-4)

Eph. 5:8-14

1. We begin in the middle of this text in order to set up the analogy of light and darkness. Besides the matchups in the Student Book, you and the class should think of others. Following are suggested answers:

Verse 8:	c	Verse 12:	a
Verse 9:	b	Verse 13:	d
Verse 11:	e		

2-3. Both references show how Christ, the Eternal Light, shines into dark hearts and ignites a new life of faith.

Eph. 5:3-7

These questions are designed for discussion, not for written answers. Have the entire class discuss them freely. Get beyond yes or no answers. Probe more deeply to "how?" and "why?"

1. God forgives all our sins, including sins against the 6th Commandment. Paul labels these sins as evidences of idolatry. Something else has replaced God. Fortunately, God forgives this idolatry. But when we persist in it, we risk losing our faith being condemned. It is not the sin that damns; it is the lack of faith.

2. **Verses 6-7** recall the Flood, the destruction of Sodom and Gomorrah, and Ananias and Sapphira.

3. Emphasize the furtive glances, the secrecy—always a sign of a dark work.

4. Emphasize and reinforce this concept. Many teenangers feel that one sin will damn them. Emphasize the direction the sinner takes after the sin. Phrases that describe this concept may be found in **vv. 8, 10, 11, 13, and 14.**

Eph. 5:15-21

The King James Version says, **"walk circumspectly"** (literally, *"with eyes all around"*) **verse 15.**

1. a. One is foolish when one does not know God's will, like one who tries to assemble a machine without reading the instructions.

   b. Getting drunk dulls the senses, is a false escape, and leads to indulgence in sensuality. One can, indeed, be filled with this.

2. Thanks to God leads us to use Christian music.

3. In **Col. 3:15-16** Paul adds purposes of teaching and admonishing. Yet both of these are also motivated by a thankful heart.

4. Use your own knowledge of Christian music to guide you. Interesting discussion should result when you measure samples of current church music against Paul's yardstick.

5. **Verse 21** is so simple it is profound. Out of love for the Lord, each antagonist should give in to the other.

SECOND HALF (Objective 4)

Plan to bring cassettes or records of many kinds of Christian music to play during this activity. Also have students bring records or tapes. If no one can provide recordings, describe (and have students describe) various kinds of Christian music. Remember, though, that the "real thing" will probably lead to better discussion.

This activity could turn into a sacred music festival. Don't overlook hymnals, song books, and choir music. As you listen, emphasize **v. 21.** God would have us gladly put up with "other" music out of reverence for Christ.

FINAL WHISTLE (Objective 4)

What more fitting way to close this session than to sing. Sing along with a tape. Or, if an instrument is handy, use it. Or sing unaccompanied. Emphasize that, no matter what our ears say, God listens to hearts and is pleased when they sing the song of faith.

Session 30: The Ultimate Imitation

BIBLE BASIS: Eph. 3:1-6; John 17:1-26

CENTRAL TRUTH

"[Jesus prayed:] Righteous Father, though the world does not know You, I know You, and they know that You have sent Me. I have made You known to them, and will continue to make You known in order that the love You have for Me may be in them and that I Myself may be in them" (John 17:25-26).

OBJECTIVES

That the students will

1. explain again that God's grace is His undeserved kindness to humanity;

2. tell about God's grace in the life of Paul;

3. describe how from the beginning God determined to extend His grace to all, Jew and Gentile, and in Christ to make them one with Him;

4. tell about the various names given to the church;

5. identify expressions of the unity of the church as found in Christian hymns.

BACKGROUND

As the final example of how "called-out ones" are imitators of God, we will see how in unity they demonstrate the oneness of God's love. This session focuses on the way God intends this unity to be. Session 31 will focus on how sin has caused this unity in the church to be shattered.

In this session we do not categorize the church into congregations, denominations, or associations. Christ has not provided a plan or directive for the formation of congregations or denominations. They occurred out of necessity and as a result of sin.

The first question of "Second Half" calls for you to provide definitions of terms. This guide provides some suggestions. You might want to check your reference books for additional insights.

Pray that your students will grow in their understanding of God's message to them and, therefore, in unity with one another and with others in the Christian church.

WARM-UP

Spend just enough time on this section to whet appetites for what the *ultimate imitation* is.

FIRST HALF (Objectives 1-3)

Eph. 3:1-6

Eph. 3 contains a huge parenthetical statement (**vv. 2-13**). Paul ponders God's grace to him personally, and the irony in the fact that God has been so good to him, and that now he is a prisoner. He then muses on the greater grace of bringing Jews and Gentiles into unity in Christ. His original thought then continues with **verse 14.**

1. God's grace came to Paul later in life as Christ personally called him to be an apostle, converting him on the road to Damascus.

2. The references listed here all refer to incidents when the Lord came to Paul in special revelations. God

revealed that he wants everyone to be saved and to come into unity with Him.

3. The great mystery as expressed here (v. 6) is this: "Through the gospel the Gentiles are heirs together with Israel, members together of one body, and sharers together in the promise in Christ Jesus."

4. The progression of references here is designed to show that God has planned salvation for all from the beginning.

    a. Gen. 12:2-3: "All peoples on earth will be blessed through you." (Reference to Christ, the greatest of Abraham's children.)

    b. Is. 60:1-3: "Nations will come to your light." (Gentiles also will become children of the light.)

    c. Matt. 8:5-12: "[Jesus said:] Many will come from the east and the west, and will take their places at the feast with Abraham, Isaac and Jacob in the kingdom of heaven." (Gentiles, like the Roman officer, take their place by faith, just as Abraham, Isaac, and Jacob did.)

    d. John 10:14-16: "[Jesus said:] I have other sheep . . . not of this sheep pen. I must bring them also. . . . there shall be one flock and one shepherd." (These other sheep are obviously the Gentiles.)

    e. Luke 24:45-48: "Repentance and forgiveness will be preached in His name to all nations." (The actual command to go out and witnesses to all)

    f. Acts 11:11-18: "God has granted even the Gentiles repentance unto life." (Paul is doing just that as he announces the answer to the great mystery in Eph. 3:6.)

5. The ultimate imitation is being "one body," and "sharers together in the promise in Christ Jesus." As God is One, so also His "called-out ones" are to be one with Christ and with each other.

John 17

The *High-Priestly Prayer* contains a beautiful expression of the unity Christ desired for His church. Have this read orally—slowly and thoughtfully—and let the magnitude of Jesus' thoughts overwhelm you.

1. Students should find a thought in vv. 1-5 or in vv. 7-8 and 10.

2. Verses 13-19 show how the disciples were human images of Christ, their teacher.

3. Verses 20-23 express this indescribable unity that we have with Him and He with us.

4. In v. 24 Christ wants His church to be with Him "where I am." This does not mean only in heaven later on. Christ now fills all things, ruling and directing the events of time. That is where His church is to be also—in the world, in time, doing His work of love. He does the ruling; we do the loving through our witness.

SECOND HALF (Objectives 4-5)

1. These terms are included here because they are widely used. Have students write your explanations in the margins, on a separate sheet of paper, or in a religion notebook.

The Holy Christian Church is holy in the sense of being made holy through the death of Christ. (God's righteousness imparted to us.)

The Communion of Saints is a fellowship of "called-out ones." This term implies the daily gathering together as family; a congregation.

The Holy Catholic Church is the universal church. (That's what "catholic" means.) It includes "called-out ones" of all time and in all places.

The Invisible Church is invisible in the sense that individual "called-out ones" do not always know who other "called-out ones" are. This term suggests that we should concentrate on witnessing instead of evaluating.

The Kingdom of Grace refers to the rule of Christ who controls with His love, not force.

The Church Militant means the church is at war with Satan. In eternity the Church Militant becomes the Church Triumphant.

2. For this activity provide copies of *Lutheran Worship* or *The Lutheran Hymnal*. Use "The Church's One Foundation" as a sample. This should direct students to the correct section of the hymnal. Have them write their

answers in their books and allow time for sharing responses.

FINAL WHISTLE
Close by singing "The Church's One Foundation" or another stirring hymn on the church.

Make assignments now for **"Final Whistle"** in session 31.

Session 31: Many Imitations

BIBLE BASIS: Eph. 3:7–13; Col. 2:16–19; Rom. 16:17–19; 1 John 4:1–3

CENTRAL TRUTH
Even though the invisible church is unified in Christ, outwardly the visible church is divided into various groups. Divisions occur because of sin. But even with divisions, the Holy Spirit still accomplishes His will. He empowers us to **"test the spirits to see whether they are from God" (1 John 4:1)** and to carry out the church's ministry.

OBJECTIVES
That the students will
1. describe how the church has been outwardly divided into denominations;
2. explain that Satan always tries to divide what God wants unified;
3. explain Paul's criteria for the evidence of the church;
4. use Paul's criteria to evaluate various denominations.

BACKGROUND
This final session on imitating God concludes the concept of unity.

Again and again in the church's history its members have felt embarrassed by the fact that it has splintered into so many denominations. To many these divisions seem incongruous with the unity Jesus prayed for in **John 17** and that Paul described in **Eph. 4** and elsewhere.

During this session we do not point fingers of accusation at those who divide. We all do this when we sin. Rather, we will see that, even though sin does divide the visible church, the Holy Spirit still empowers this divided body to carry on His work.

During **"Second Half"** students are asked to analyze how various denominations carry on this work. To help them work though this activity, you will need to provide information about the denominations they identify. Check resources such as *Handbook of Denominations in the United States* by Frank S. Mead and Samuel S. Hill; *My Church and Others* by J. T. Mueller; *Creeds of the Churches* by J. H. Leith; *Larson's Book of Cults* by Bob Larson; *The Kingdom of the Cults* by Walter Martin; and *The Four Major Cults* by A. A. Hoekema. All these are available through Concordia Publishing House.

Individuals will need to prepare in advance for the prayer suggestions in **"Final Whistle."** Consider making these assignments at the end of session 30.

Pray that the Holy Spirit will keep your students faithful to Christ and His teachings about Himself, about sin and grace, about Scripture, and about Himself.

WARM-UP (Objective 1)
The diagram used here is adapted from *Catechetical Helps* by Erwin Kurth. It tries to show how major divisions have occurred. Introduce the term *denomination* as a religious organization that unites local congregations into a legal and administrative body. Do not go too deeply into the history of denominations. Explain just enough to demonstrate the fact of denominationalism.

Conclude this part by stressing the two points made. Recognize that there are believers in all true Christian denominations **(Is. 55:11)** and that sin is the element that keeps denominations divided.

FIRST HALF (Objectives 2–3)
1. Quickly discuss the three Old Testament examples cited. Move then to those from the early church.
a. Greek and Jewish believers were divided over the distribution of food.

b. Peter and Paul were divided over to relate to the Gentiles. Paul accused Peter of being two-faced.

c. Paul and Barnabas split up over what to do about John Mark, who **had deserted them at Perga during** the first missionary journey.

d. The Corinthian Christians were **divided into factions based on** who had brought God's Word to them.

You might discuss whether these disagreements were really important. **At times Satan splits up the visible** church over insignificant questions. Use your experience to recall some examples for the class.

2. Following are suggested answers to these questions:

a. **Eph. 3:7-11:** God intends for the church to proclaim the manifold wisdom of God (the story of salvation) to all humanity. **"Rulers and authorities in the heavenly realms" (v. 10)** may refer to angels, who also have a vital interest in the story of salvation. (See 1 Peter 1:12.)

b. **Col. 2:16-19:** The one out of control is the one who teaches falsely. That person is like a part of the body that is disconnected from the head and is therefore no longer part of the body.

c. **Rom. 16:17-19:** Those who cause divisions and erect obstacles are those who are disconnected. They are out of sync with the plain teaching of Scripture ("the teaching you have learned"—v. 17).

d. **1 John 4:1-3:** Each teaching or evidence of it (spirit) is to be evaluated on whether it ultimately glorifies Christ (both His human and divine natures). All false doctrine will in some way take away from the work of Christ for us.

3. Which denomination is the right one? Obviously, we feel that The Lutheran Church—Missouri Synod is the correct one. Otherwise we wouldn't be in it. Nevertheless, have students use Paul's declaration of purpose in **Eph. 3:7-13** to evaluate it objectively.

Students who are members of another denomination may evaluate that one instead.

Note that a, c, d, and e refer to key doctrines God has given to His church. The others (b and f) refer to responses we make to God. Teachings elsewhere in Scripture accent other responses (e.g., worship in **Eph. 5:19-20**).

a. We need to recognize humanity's utter spiritual helplessness and the fact that God's salvation is solely His work **("through the working of His power" Eph. 3:7)**

b. The church should proclaim God's grace in Christ to all people.

c. The church's message is based on the manifold wisdom of God (God's Word). Paul mentions that what it proclaims is of interest to angels.

d. All of God's plan and purpose is wrapped up in Christ. Everything a denomination does should begin and end in Christ.

e. We receive God's grace solely through faith in Christ—not through faith in goodness, self, or anything else.

f. Suffering is a part of the glory of being sons and daughters of God.

SECOND HALF (Objective 4)

This activity is vital since it touches students in daily life. Do this as a class activity. Use the board to list criteria as headings. Then list denominations members of your class suggest. Evaluate each of them. Pay special attention to the crucial doctrines represented in a, c, d, and e.

Point out the need to use these criteria to evaluate a local congregation. In spite of official pronouncements of a denomination, it is the local congregation where the actual practice of these six criteria are best seen.

This analysis will show that the Holy Spirit does work through all true Christian denominations. Individual Christians will want to affiliate with the denomination that does the best job of being the church.

FINAL WHISTLE

Assign one session each, 26–31, to six students. Have them quickly reread the material and then include the needs of each session in a short prayer for use at the end of this session.

Session 32: Witnessing by Giving

BIBLE BASIS: 2 Cor. 8:1–15

CENTRAL TRUTH

Members of the church imitate God in the grace of giving. God's undeserved kindness moves us to respond by giving Him ourselves and our possessions.

OBJECTIVES

That the students will

1. tell how the church today appears to be one of many groups that want money;

2. identify God's gift of salvation through Christ as the only motivation for true giving;

3. use Paul's guidelines to evaluate fund-raising techniques.

BACKGROUND

Read the Student Book and Teachers Guide for session 33 of *God's Old Testament People* (a 9th-grade course in the Lutheran High School Religion Series) for background material on the topic of this session.

Giving is a fruit of faith that gives a strong witness to the new life in Christ. Even though not all teenagers have jobs, they all have money. One might be surprised to find out how miserly young people are. Yes, they do spend money, but mostly on themselves. The grace of giving does not develop naturally outside of God's Word.

Again and again teenagers see evidence of the power of money in our society. They probably even see how much importance their local congregation and their school give to money, especially if you conduct fund-raising activities each year.

Use this session to continue to build groundwork for Christian giving that was provided in session 33 of *God's Old Testament People*. You may touch a sensitive nerve when you discuss fund-raising. There should not really be a conflict, however, for when

our heart belongs to Christ, so does the wallet.

Pray that God's love for your students will cause them to respond in love to Him. **"He died for all, that those who live should no longer live for themselves but for Him who died for them and was raised again" (2 Cor. 5:15).**

WARM-UP (Objective 1)

The story presented merely intends to put Christian giving in the context where most of us find it—one of many demands on our pocketbooks. Allow the students to speculate on the contents of the last three envelopes. The "Office of the Auditor" could have been one of the many computer-written ads informing you "personally" that you have won a "gift."

Students probably won't disagree with Mrs. Anderson's comments about the letter from the congregation. They've probably heard comments like that all too often. Therefore move right into the reading. Make sure the students realize that God does say quite a bit about giving.

FIRST HALF (Objective 2)

This reading should be fairly easy to understand. But be ready to explain difficult passages. As you discuss, you might begin with **verse 9** as follows:

a. **Verse 9:** The prime motivation for giving comes from love for Christ, who emptied Himself for our sakes.

b. **Verse 5:** When we accept **verse 9** by faith, we will then empty ourselves by giving ourselves to the Lord.

c. **Verses 2–3:** The motivation from **verse 9** creates this overwhelming desire to give.

d. **Verse 4:** Love for God moves us to show love to fellow saints.

e. **Verse 8:** God does not want us to

give as a result of force, be it physical or social, but only out of love, as Paul says.

True–False Statements

Spend most of your time discussing why statements are true or false.

1. **True.** The congregation at Philippi, in particular, is well known for supporting Paul and contributing to the needs of the Christians in Jerusalem. This occurred even though persecution and hardships plagued the area.

2. **False.** The Macedonian congregations gave because they gave themselves first to the Lord. Giving in response to a plea does not always imply a heart given first to the Lord.

3. **True.** See #2. One cannot give his or her heart and withhold income and possessions, which go with the body.

4. **True.** In **verse 7b** Paul speaks of the **grace of giving.** Giving by definition is then a result of undeserved kindness. When we hope to get a return for a gift, we are speaking of a business deal, not of grace.

5. **False.** Titus (**v. 6**) was merely a gatherer of gifts, not a fund-raiser. The church is to gather the gifts (fruits of faith) shaken out of the tree by the Wind of God (the Holy Spirit).

6. **True.** **Verse 7** repeats the list of spiritual gifts discussed elsewhere (**1 Cor. 12:1–11; Rom. 12:3–8**). Giving is one of them, again motivated solely by God's grace.

7. **True/False.** The statement is true as far as it goes. But it doesn't state the gross imbalance of **verse 9.** Christ not only gave from His richness, but actually gave it all up, becoming poor (His human nature) so that we could become God's sons and daughters (our eternal inheritance).

8. **False.** Paul was not speaking about competition. He was gently reminding them to finish what they started (**vv. 10–11**). The idea of giving to win a prize for being the most generous does not fit with 2 Cor. 9:7.

9. **True.** **Verse 13** indicates that when God has blessed us with more than we need, that is perhaps a signal that there is someone with whom we can share. *False* becomes an acceptable answer if a student uses logic such as, "Paul expected the Corinthians to give up their possessions to demonstrate their response to God's love for them."

10. **True.** Paul is recalling a quote from **Exodus** concerning manna. God still sends manna, but the delivery truck is His church.

11. **False.** While we will want to focus on the idea of responding to God's love in Christ, Christian leadership may also suggest guidelines for giving. Nowhere did Jesus, Paul, or others tell us to set aside the Old Testament guidelines for tithing.

Unfinished Sentences

This activity is optional. If you had lots of fruitful discussion in connection with the quiz, omit this activity. If, however, you would like to have the students express their understandings personally, then ask them to complete these sentences.

SECOND HALF   (Objective 3)

Probably not everyone will be pleased when you touch the shrine of the sacred cow of fund-raising, but that subject must be addressed. Review once more Paul's five steps in giving (listed above at the beginning of E"First Half"). You might want to write them on the board.

Use this activity to bring giving habits into conformity with those of the Lord. No doubt, pet projects will come under examination. Some of your congregation's and school's fund-raising techniques may be questioned. And they should be if they discourage people from giving out of love for God. **Every** effort must seek to develop cheerful givers, not people who give reluctantly or under compulsion.

Since each situation is unique, this guide will not try to pass judgment on them (though a raffle seems *very* questionable). Feel free to add more techniques as they are mentioned.

FINAL WHISTLE

If those hymnals are still around, close by reading or singing "We Give You But Your Own" (*LW* 405, *TLH* 441).

Session 33: Witnessing by Receiving

BIBLE BASIS: Phil. 4:4-7, 10-20

CENTRAL TRUTH

God, who gives us all good gifts, empowers us to witness by the way we receive those gifts. He moves us to show thanks, praise, and contentment, even in times of trouble.

OBJECTIVES

That the students will

1. describe the difficulty people have in receiving compliments and gifts;

2. recall and put into practice Paul's three marks of God-pleasing receiving: recognizing God as Giver; being satisfied with His gifts; rejoicing in His goodness;

3. look for God's blessings in even difficult situations.

BACKGROUND

As we have seen, the church has been quite concerned with the giving habits of its members. This session deals with another important topic: **receiving God's gifts.** Our sinful human nature may lead us to feel guilt when we receive a gift from someone but do not give one in return. Or we may want to *pay for* a gift. We in the church may be tempted to want to pay for *God's* gifts, hoping we can induce Him to produce more. At times like these we, with Paul, must recognize that salvation and all its accompanying gifts are free through the work of Christ.

"Called-out ones" also need to recognize God's blessings even in difficult situations. Be sure to point out that death, evil, and trouble do not originate with God. Satan is their author and dispenser. God, however, often uses Satan's bombs to build up His children.

Before class plan the compliments you will pass around during **"Warm-Up."**

Pray that the Holy Spirit will move your students to recognize God as the Giver of all good gifts, to feel satisfied with whatever they receive from Him, and to rejoice in His goodness, even in tough situations.

WARM-UP (Objective 1)

Plan an activity in which every student in your class receives a compliment. To begin, think of an honest reason to praise each person. You might compliment them individually on their cooperation, their punctuality, their cheerfulness, etc. Whatever the compliment, make sure it is genuine. If you wish, also allow a few minutes for students to compliment one another.

This activity then leads into the observation that we (teachers included) have trouble handling compliments and gifts. Go directly into **Phil. 4.**

FIRST HALF (Objectives 2-3)

Phil. 4:13

Paul's **"I can do everything"** might include:
Believe in God
Remain faithful to Him
Keep hold of my temper (Acts 13:10-11; Gal. 5:12)
Preach the Good News
Run a good race (Phil. 3:12-14)

Accept any response that indicates the Spirit of God at work. These references to Paul also describe what God can do through us.

Phil. 4:10-12, and 14-20

You might ask students to take notes in advance on a separate sheet of paper. They could form discussion groups to discuss the passages.

1. By feeling contentment in each situation, Paul showed complete trust in the loving providence of God.

a. After Paul's confrontation with Christ, he was physically blind and spiritually disoriented. Ananias then assured him of God's peace and baptized him.

b. After the stoning at Lystra, some friends cared for him, revived him, and sent him on his way.

c. Lydia, a wealthy business woman, took Paul and Silas in and cared for them.

d. Apparently Paul was suffering from his illness when he arrived in Galatia. These people cared for him as a messenger of God.

e. Along with the other survivors of the shipwreck, Paul was saved from death.

2. Students should make the following ovservations:

a. Certainly Paul's former life as a Pharisee indicated being well off statuswise if not materially.

b. Luke reports that in Rome under house arrest, Paul lived a quite normal life.

c. After receiving the Philippian gift, Paul sounds as if he had few physical needs. This may have been while he was also under house arrest in Rome (Acts 28:30–31).

3. Paul's secret: "I can do everything through Him who gives me strength" (v. 13).

Phil. 4:4–7

1. Paul's expresses his happiness with God in v. 4: "Rejoice in the Lord always. I will say it again: Rejoice!"

2. The words of verse 7 are sometimes referred to as the votum and used as the blessing after the sermon. The peace of God transcends all understanding.

SECOND HALF (Objective 3)

Both activities point out that we should, as Paul said, rejoice always! Even when things are going bad.

1. If you used discussion groups for "First Half," you might have these same group consider each situation and speculate how God can turn each tragedy into blessing. Don't be content with one blessing. Overspeculate as to what God can do.

In addition, each group should come up with one or two more situations from their experiences where God could also bring blessing from disaster.

2. These minor difficulties, when viewed from the top side of eternity, can also bring blessings to the owners.

FINAL WHISTLE

As a concluding devotion, list on the board some of the minor problems and the blessings that came from them. For these, as did Paul, give thanks publicly.

Session 34: Where Do Our Gifts Go?

BIBLE BASIS: Matt. 25:31–40

CENTRAL TRUTH

Our faith in God and our love from Him moves us to give good gifts to those in need. When we do this, we are really giving those gifts to the Lord Jesus.

OBJECTIVES

That the students will

1. state the purpose for the church's witness;

2. identify the basis for salvation;

3. identify people or groups who have represented Christ to those around them;

4. explain that what we do for others is really done for Christ;

5. express a commitment to help those in need.

BACKGROUND

This session focuses on the effects of the gifts we give to others. In Matt. 25 Jesus Himself describes events of the Last Day. We find a reference with more description and without dialog in 1 Thess. 4:13–18.

Matt. 25 clearly shows that when God moves us to act out of love for others, we really show love to the Lord Himself. Because this is true, we need not feel concerned that the money and other aid we give for the poor and destitute might be wasted. While we do want our gifts to accomplish the goals we have for them, God has already accomplished His gift through us.

Verses 41–46 are not included in this session. This was done to avoid getting sidetracked into the subject of what happens to the lost. As Scripture teaches, the lost are damned because of their rejection of God's grace. Such rejection will not produce works done for God's glory.

Pray that God will open the hearts

of your students to demonstrate His love to those in need around them.

WARM-UP (Objective 1)

Quickly read through this section, focusing again on the real reason for the church's witness. The three reasons given in the second paragraph should never be the main reason for our work.

FIRST HALF (Objectives 2-4)

Matt. 25:31-34

The term *Judgment Day* is misleading in that it implies that each person's eternal destiny is in doubt, and that Christ the Judge will on that day weigh the evidence presented and render the verdict of eternal life or death.

Being a "called-out one" means that each individual has his or her name already written in the Book of Life. Christ's activity is therefore more of a separation. Publicly He will designate who are His "called-out ones."

The parable referred to here pictures "called-out ones" as wheat and unbelievers as weeds. In this life both grow together, but on "Harvest Day" God separates us.

1. On the basis of Christ knowing us as "called out ones" He separates us from weeds. It is entirely His choice.

2. Jesus says in **verse 34, "Take your inheritance, the kingdom prepared for you since the creation of the world."** In **Matt.** 13:27 the servant (angel) refers to the wheat seeds as "good." We are good in the sense that God has counted us righteous for Jesus' sake.

3. All these passages show that we are saved by God's work, not ours.

Matt. 25:35-40

1. Jesus here refers to six curses that resulted from sin: hunger, thirst, loneliness, nakedness, sickness (pain), and violence. He Himself, as true man, experienced all of them. You might ask the class to recall when.

2. The field is wide open on this activity. Use the current need situation to answer these.

3. Paul's versions of Jesus' lesson are as follows:

a. **Rom.** 12:1: Offer yourselves as living sacrifices to God.

b. **1 Cor.** 10:31: All we do should be done for the glory of God.

c. **2 Cor.** 8:5: The Macedonians gave themselves first to the Lord.

d. **Gal.** 4:14: The Galatians welcomed Paul as an angel and even as Christ.

e. **Eph.** 6:5: Workers are to work as if Christ were the boss.

f. **Col.** 3:17: Whatever we do, do it all in the name (as representatives) of the Lord.

4. Rather than asking students to share the paragraphs they wrote, you might ask them to use this as a basis for silent meditation and prayer at the end of this class session. Ask students to express a commitment and to ask for God's help in living and sharing their faith with others.

SECOND HALF (Objective 5)

One cannot read **Matt. 25** without applying the list of human needs to the current situation. That is the purpose of this activity.

The questions and phrases are designed to stimulate thinking about those in need. Plan to hold a class-wide discussion of these issues.

Begin by identifying those in need. Then discuss the prospect of supplying help. Your class (or groups within the class) might choose to undertake some charitable work. Encourage them to visit a convalescent home, collect food and clothing, write letters to prisoners, contribute to one of the many world hunger drives, etc. We certainly cannot say that Christ does not appear to us in the guise of the needy.

FINAL WHISTLE

After discussing the many examples of those in need, it seems logical to conclude this session with prayers for them. Or you might ask students to meditate on the thoughts they wrote in the last "First Half" activity. If you have a mature and sharing group, develop a litany with students' prayer requests.

Session 35: Concluding Activities for Unit 5

The 14 sessions in this unit covered the general topic of witnessing by Word and deed. Sessions 21–25 covered witnessing by Word and sessions 26–34 covered witnessing by deed.

To prepare for this review, read again all the central truths and objectives. Reread also the main texts of each session. Then look again at the study material for each text. Finally, reread the activities that you covered in the "Second Half" portions of the sessions.

If you plan to prepare a test, base it on the larger concepts (objectives) along with some of the applications found in "Second Half."

The review in the Students Book asks them to prepare questions for the answers provided. This format provides a change from the usual "write an answer" type of review. At the same time it provides a vehicle for summarizing main points.

Following are questions you might use:

1. Outline Jesus' plan for those who will speak for Him.
2. Supply eight examples of people whose lives were changed by the Spirit.
3. What is the message of **John 4?**
4. List three devices Jesus used in **John 4.** What do they represent?
5. How can a Christian congregation do more witnessing than an individual can do?
6. How was Ephesus then like the world is today?
7. What is a synod and why is it formed?
8. How does the church imitate God?
9. Explain Paul's analogy of Christ and the church.
10. How is a person's life after conversion like a new garment?
11. What is the difference between people of the light and people of the dark?
12. How did Jesus express His desire for unity for His followers? Where do you find these words of Jesus?
13. Describe the test for the evaluation of a denomination given in **Eph. 3:7–13.**
14. What makes a gift acceptable to our Lord?
15. How is Jesus the true receiver of the gifts of the church?

Permission is herewith granted duplicate the above questions for testing or review. Please add the following credit line: Publishing House copyright 1987. Used by permission.

Unit 6: Conflict and Victory

The church's enemies (the devil, the sinful world, and our sinful flesh) oppose the rightful use of all the gifts God has showered on the church plus all the church's responses to those gifts.

Unit 6 exposes those enemies in the context in which they operate. But we also look at the help we receive from God. Your students will receive the spiritual equipment needed for a victorious life.

Finally, Christ's victory on the church's behalf is celebrated here and in heaven. We give the students a peek into eternity to catch the joy of the eternal celebration.

The unit concludes with a special worship service and some material for review.

Session 36: Recognizing the Enemy

BIBLE BASIS: Selected references

CENTRAL TRUTH

The enemy of the church is Satan, the sinful world, and our sinful flesh.

The church needs to be on guard against attacks from these three. Through Christ we already have assurance of victory in this battle.

OBJECTIVES

That the students will

1. describe the importance of the struggle for their lives;

2. describe how Satan has operated throughout time and how he has been defeated by Christ;

3. explain how the struggle is conducted in their lives;

4. identify weapons that Satan uses.

BACKGROUND

Your students undoubtedly have heard of Satan and remember many Bible stories where he is involved. But they might not realize how deeply Satan is involved in their lives. Some more sophisticated students may have even consigned Satan to the status of a childhood "closet monster" or "the bogeyman." Help them recognize that Satan remains **very** active today. Often this crafty enemy disguises himself so we're not really aware of the way he's tempting us, as he tempts us through our closest friends. At other times, as when we are invited to participate in Satan worship, his temptations are more obvious.

This session presents the eternally serious consequences of Satan's operation. Students will see his involvement in the story of salvation. Be sure to assure them that Satan has been defeated by Christ. Satan is tempting them to join the losing side. Even so, he *is* powerful; he *will* lead us to fall if we trust in our own power. But God gives us His power; through it we *can* overcome Satan's temptations. Keep these facts in the forefront when working through "Second Half."

Pray the words of the Luther's explanation of the Sixth Petition of the Lord's Prayer for your students: **"God tempts no one. [I] pray . . . that God would guard and keep [them] so that the devil, the world, and [their] sinful nature may not deceive [them] or mislead [them] into false belief, despair, and other great shame and vice. Although [they] are attacked by these things, [I] pray that [they] may finally overcome them and win the victory."**

WARM—UP (Objective 1)

Briefly read through the unit introducton and this section. Emphasize that this is a deadly contest, with their eternal residence as the prize. Move immediately into "First Half."

FIRST HALF (Objectives 2-3)

The Struggle Then

The references selected summarize the struggle from Satan's viewpoint. Point out that Satan's temptation of Adam and Eve was designed to retaliate against God. Satan cares nothing for humanity. He tries to use our sins to hurt God.

Following are the answers:

1. h	4. g	7. d
2. f	5. i	8. b
3. c	6. e	9. a

The Struggle Now

These references bring Satan's warfare into a personal focus. St. Paul certainly was aware of Satan's efforts to thwart God's plans. Have the students read the references and formulate answers in their own words. Encourage variations in responses for discussion purposes.

1. Eph. 6:10—12: Secular rulers and authorities are those who control others. Examples include evil governments, mass thought control (advertising propaganda) economic masters (control through credit, hunger, warfare). Spiritual forces of evil are Satan and the evil spirits who make up the unseen residents of hell.

2. Rom. 8:38—39:

a. Note carefully that **nothing** will cause God to remove His love. We are the only other party. We remove ourselves from God's love when we allow temptation and sin to drive us away from Him.

b. Satan's favorite ploy is to try to convince us that God doesn't love us anymore, that we are so bad that God has given up on us. We tend to feel this way when a life of sin replaces our life in Him.

3. Rom. 7:14—25:

a. Paul found himself doing what he

knew was wrong; and not doing what what he knew he should do. Out of weakness, his sinful nature often gained the upper hand.

b. When we lose such struggles, we have only one cure available: to scurry back to the nail-pierced hands of a waiting and loving Savior, asking once again for forgiveness.

4. **2 Tim. 4:6—8:** Paul knew he was facing death at the hands of the Romans. He looked forward to death as the final step into the glory of eternity. For him it meant the end of the struggle. He and his fellow believers would then stand in the winner's circle of eternity.

SECOND HALF (Objectives 2—4)

1. Remember that whatever Satan controls is a loser no matter how it looks. The church has used the term, "unholy three," to summarize the enemies of the faith. Refer the students to the references indicated to see how Scripture pictures them.

If possible, do this activity in groups. There will be as many answers as there are groups. This activity was not designed to lead students to find a "rotten fish in every newspaper." There is much that Christians can and should enjoy. But we do need to be on the lookout for the telltale signs that Satan has left his poison.

The following is a sample of how just one category (movies) could be analyzed.

World: Show revenge and violence; glamorize sin.

Sinful Flesh: Appeal to lust;

illicit sex; emphasize "me first" attitude.

2. Talk about whatever temptations seem relevant to your students. The influx of Asians into our country has caused an influx of religions they have brought with them. Satan worship probably has much more appeal to young people than you every imagined possible. The "being good" idolatry has always been with us. For example, one might say (or at least think), "If I go to church every Sunday, and *try* to do what God tells me to do, and give some money to Him (maybe even a tithe!), and even read the Bible on my own sometimes, I can't miss! I'll surely get to heaven! I deserve it!"

3. Only God's power can overcome Satan's temptations. And only the forgiveness Jesus has earned for us can rescue us when we fall.

FINAL WHISTLE

As a way of dramatizing Satan's way of operating, read orally **Job 1:1—2:10.** Close with the reminder that he is still out there **"roaming through the earth and going back and forth in it"** (Job 1:7). If you can provide copies of Luther's explanation to the Sixth Petition of the Lord's Prayer, read it together as a closing prayer.

LOOKING AHEAD

Session 39: The last activity in "First Half" requires you to provide information about religious groups who attempt to attract followers with a false Gospel. Begin now to gather that information.

Session 37: Using Your Equipment

BIBLE BASIS: Eph. 6:13—18

CENTRAL TRUTH

The Lord equips His church with spiritual armor and weapons that enable it to defend itself against Satan's attacks.

OBJECTIVES

That the students will

1. describe the folly of not using the gifts God provides;

2. explain the background of Paul's analogy in Eph. 6:14—17;

3. apply Paul's analogy to their own lives;

4. identify daily opportunities to use the armor of God.

BACKGROUND

The armor of God may be the best-known of all the analogies Paul presents in his epistles. Roman soldiers were a common sight to first-century Christians. Paul, therefore, did not have to elaborate on the use of armor. Since 20th-century students may not have such knowledge, we have provided an introduction to such equipment. Use it to make the analogy valuable to them.

It may be more difficult, however, to demonstrate how one may use the spiritual equipment. That is the purpose of "Second Half." The underlying purpose of the entire session is to show the students that God has not left us defenseless against Satan.

Pray that God will empower your students to rely on Him when they battle Satan's temptations, using the armor He has provided for them.

WARM-UP (Objective 1)

Interested students may want to read more about this incident in U. S. history. For this session point out that only an inexperienced or absolutely stupid soldier would discard equipment. You might expand the analogy to protective equipment in football, hockey, baseball. Some students may be familiar with hard-hats, steel-toe shoes, leather gloves, reflective vests, etc. worn by construction workers and others.

FIRST HALF (Objectives 1-3)

Use this section to provide understanding of the text itself and of the analogy Paul uses there.

1. A soldier who discards one piece of equipment becomes that much more vulnerable. When a soldier is not fully equipped, he or she becomes a weaker part of a fighting force.

2. We can think of the "day of evil" as any time Satan comes with temptations (in other words--always).

3. Think of this spiritual warfare as a matter of conquering and maintaining the hearts of people. The ground to be controlled is the heart and soul of the believer. As long as "the called-out one" is standing, he or she is still Christ's property. When the "called-out one" succumbs to temptation, that heart is in danger of being taken over by Satan.

4. The purpose of labeling the diagram is not to test the ability of

your students, but to help them get into the thinking of the first century. The short descriptions of the uses of the Roman soldier's equipment have the same purpose.

Paul's comment in **verse 18** is worthy of note: Good soldiers are in constant communication with headquarters. They know their orders and follow them to the letter. Good soldiers also realize they are a part of a much larger group. Their actions therefore are determined on the basis of what is best for the entire group.

5. Have the entire class carefully work out the responses. Allow them to *struggle* making the connections. Don't supply the answer until you are convinced the class can't. The value here is in *struggling* for the answer. They should try to visualize what would happen if each of God's gifts was gone.

As students work, they will undoubtedly recognize that they often fail to rely completely on God's armor. Emphasize the Gospel truths presented in the references. God provides the power; we don't. He also provides His grace, the complete forgiveness of every sin one of His children commits.

a. This provides a sample of how students can make the connection.

b. The heart of our faith is in the righteousness, earned by Christ, but credited to us. Satan aims for a mortal blow to convince us that we have to do something to earn it.

c. We can't continue to stand unless our shoes supply support and protection. The Good News always provides the comfort and support that we need to survive in rocky, unfriendly places.

d. Believing in God, whom we have not seen, and trusting Him for everything, will--like a shield--absorb and deflect those pesky doubts, fears, and worries that could wear us down.

e. Knowing that we are God's sons and daughters, that Jesus has saved us, is like a helmet that keeps us from losing consciousness.

f. God provides His Word as the offensive weapon to fight against temptation. Satan must bow to it. That is why we need to know it and to practice using it. Notice that this was the weapon Jesus used to defeat Satan's temptations.

SECOND HALF (Objective 4)

Use the answers from #5 above to provide armor for the six situations. We need all types of armor in each situation. Try to determine which piece is used the most. Following are some possible solutions.

1. *Helmet of Salvation*. We know that God has made us His children for this life and heirs of an even better life yet to come.

2. *Shoes of the Gospel*. Christ provides all the goodness we need for salvation; we don't need to earn it. This fact might even show our friends that we can't be a goody-goodie. The only perfect one is Christ.

3. *Shield of Faith*. Without faith in a loving God, such disasters could convince us that there is nothing to live for. The shield of faith shows us that God can use troubles to strengthen that faith.

4. *Breastplate of Righteousness*. Satan would hope that after being caught we would believe that God would never forgive us. But that's not true, because we wear *His* righteousness.

5. *The Belt of Truth*. We're not likely to convince unbelievers just because we know exactly what God has said and done. God does use our knowledge of the truth, however, to keep us from falling into compromises and error.

6. *The Sword of the Spirit*. Here is the perfect spot to use God's Word—not to condemn others, or explain our life, but to show how doing things Christ's way is His gift of the new life. More on this in the next session.

FINAL WHISTLE

Suggest that each student silently talk to the Lord about increasing his or her use of God's armor. Pray particularly for help in any area where Satan's temptations seem to be especially strong.

Session 38: The Sword of the Spirit

BIBLE BASIS: Matt. 4:1–17; 1 Cor. 2:1–16; Heb. 4:12–13

CENTRAL TRUTH

God gives the church the sword of the Spirit (the Word of God) to defend itself against the temptations of Satan. This two-edged sword consists of Law and Gospel.

OBJECTIVES

That the students will

1. explain that the Word of God, as our only weapon against Satan, demonstrates God's power, not ours;

2. describe the power of the Word, as it is the vehicle for the Spirit to work among us;

3. identify the qualities of Law and Gospel;

4. recognize Law and Gospel in Scripture.

BACKGROUND

Continuing Paul's analogy of spiritual armor from **Eph. 6**, this session focuses on the **sword of the Spirit** (the Word of God). Law and Gospel were presented earlier in connection with witnessing. Certainly fighting against Satan's temptations is a type of witnessing. The emphasis here, however, is to show how God's word can be used to fight against Satan. "Second Half" gives the students practice in identifying Law and Gospel in Scripture.

Pray that God will give you the wisdom to apply Law and Gospel properly in your classroom, and that He will bless your efforts.

WARM-UP

The four statements presented are intended to arouse some curiosity about Paul's use of the term *sword of the Spirit*. Each is explained later in the session.

FIRST HALF (Objectives 1–4)

Matt. 4:1–17

The first statement seems logical: "The more weapons one has the better." Not so. Christ, as shown, had innumerable weapons at His disposal.

1. Jesus refers here (Matt. 26:52–54) to over 72,000 angels, quite a weapon when you consider what one angel can do.

2. The emphasis here (John 18:36) is that Jesus' kingdom is not of this world, but "is from another place." This other place (heaven) is not subject to physical laws and would be a most formidable foe.

3. Referring again to Christ's classic struggle with Satan, help your students find the Old Testament references:

    a. Deut. 8:3.
    b. Deut. 6:16.
    c. Deut. 6:13.

Make the point that in each quote Christ reminds Satan that God is in charge, and that Satan also must obey.

4. If we battled Satan, using God's power as we willed, we would probably take the credit. As it is, we recognize that Satan is defeated entirely through God's power and will.

1 Cor. 2

In this reference Paul allows us to see him in action.

1. See v. 3. Paul apparently was not a great orator. People were not swayed by technique, but by the power of the Spirit.

2. See vv. 11–12, 14. Only through the Spirit can God's will and God's grace be understood. Without the Spirit, we cannot understand or believe anything about God.

3. Paul certainly could not rely on his own power (v. 4). His power came from the Spirit of God contained in the Word of God. Paul was a master at wielding this sword.

Heb. 4:12–13

Take time to outline on the board the qualities of the Law and Gospel. Make clear that both Law and Gospel are found in both Old and New Testaments, often side by side.

As you proceed with "Second Half," be aware that it is impossible to isolate many passages as strictly Law or Gospel. For example, in John 15:12 Jesus say, "My command is this: . . ".

Taken out of context this would certainly be Law. But read in context the passage is pure Gospel––"as I have loved you." We can only obey Jesus command to love after we have been enfolded in His love. We often make Gospel into Law by taking what is a gift of God's grace and saying, "Now we should . . . ." Actually, as God's love motivates us to live the new life, the Spirit lives and works through us, a sign of the Gospel.

The analogy presented is not intended to dwell on the mechanics of swordplay, but on the two directions of power, Law and Gospel. Perhaps thinking of the Gospel as destructive is foreign to our thinking. But the Gospel does destroy our pride in our own accomplishments.

The answers to Jesus' quotes are:

1. Gospel; our life is totally dependent on God's breath of life.

2. Law; this echoes Heb. 3:7–9, where Israel tried the Lord's patience.

3. Law; a repeat of the First Commandment.

SECOND HALF (Objectives 3–4)

1. Use your own discretion in working through these references. Try not to get wrapped up in the story or larger frame of reference. Just determine whether mostly Law or Gospel is presented. Following are possible designations:

a. John 3:16; Gospel entirely.

b. Matt. 5:3–10: Gospel. In Matthew's Gospel the word "blessed" indicates that God is working by His grace for our good.

c. Matt. 5:38–39; Law.

d. John 14:2–4: Gospel, all action for us.

e. Acts 2:36: Pure Law. Peter says, "whom you crucified." A perfect illustration of the Law convicting the listener of sin. Note the effect in v. 37.

f. Is. 9:2: Gospel.

g. Is. 9:19: Law.

h. Ezek. 34:1–4: Law (reference to the wicked spiritual leadership of Judah).

i. Ezek. 34:11–16: Gospel, prefiguring the Good Shepherd.

j. 2 Peter 3:8–9: Gospel; shows God's great mercy and long suffering.

k. 2 Peter 3:10: Law; next verse shows violent end to physical world.

l. **James 1:25:** Gospel. The law that gives freedom is our faith in Christ which blesses all our works with God's approval.

m. **Gen. 3:15:** Gospel; the first promise of a Savior.

n. **Rev. 22:18–19:** Law; a threat to would-be "editors."

2. Give students some time to think about this activity. Then encourage (but do not insist on) discussion about the way the Law helps them. Reinforce responses that make very specific applications, but respect fully the right to remain silent.

3. After students have had time to think about the Gospel promises, divide the class into pairs to share their promises. If time permits, allow a few students to share the sweetness of the Gospel with the entire class.

FINAL WHISTLE
A closing prayer by the instructor, requesting guidance and success in using God's Word, would be most appropriate.

Session 39: The Great Battle

BIBLE BASIS: Luke 21:5–19;
2 Thess. 2:1–12

CENTRAL TRUTH
God warns us about a fierce struggle between Christ's church and the forces of Satan. God reminds us to be prepared, and He promises to grant us victory in the struggle.

OBJECTIVES
That the students will

1. explain Christ's references to the warfare that His disciples would wage against Satan;

2. identify instances within memory where these struggles have taken place;

3. identify evidences of the spirit of lawlessness that is present now;

4. formulate their own responses to spiritual attacks on their own faith.

BACKGROUND
The topic of this session calls for a reading of prophecy from the New Testament. When reading prophecy we are tempted to pinpoint events and personalities, to become nothing more than religious fortune-tellers. God always gives prophecy to sustain and increase faith in our victorious Savior.

The text from **Luke** refers to the events the disciples would encounter after Christ's ascension. As we know from **Acts,** the disciples indeed did suffer persecutions, imprisonments, and even death. Perhaps Luke, as he wrote, recalled much of this happening to Paul, his companion.

In the **Thessalonians** text Paul himself divulges information that appears nowhere else in his letters. As indicated, the Thessalonians were confused about a letter erroneously ascribed to Paul, that stated that Christ had returned and that they had missed Him (v. 2).

Paul's references to the **"man of lawlessness" (v. 3)** clearly refers to a physical being, not just Satan. Do not get into a "Who is this man?" guessing game. Focus on what he does, and not on his identity. Every age, it seems, has a spirit of lawlessness that batters at the very foundations of faith.

The last activity in **"First Half"** requires the use of ads or information about people who would lead us toward false Christs. **Look for information to bring to class for this activity. Also alert students to look for information you can use.**

Pray for perseverance in the struggle with Satan. Ask God to keep you and all your students faithful to Him.

WARM-UP
We return to the athletic theme. Probably many students will have painful memories of these little jewels. Make the point that the drill focuses on some vital skill that is needed in the real contest.

Following are the suggested purposes for the activities listed:

1. Change of direction, conditioning

2. Dexterity, recovery, and conditioning

3. Conditioning, pacing

4. Facility in vocabulary and sentence structure

5. Knowledge and skill "under fire"

Make the transition to our preparing for a great spiritual struggle.

FIRST HALF (Objectives 1-3)

Luke 21:5-19

1. Through deception, some will claim to be Christ or to know when He will return.

2. **Acts 4:1-5:** Peter and John were arrested.

Acts 6:8—7:60: Stephen testified before the Jews and was killed.

Acts 8:1-3: Persecutions in Jerusalem, many headed by Saul (St. Paul).

Acts 12:1-18: Peter's arrest and escape.

Acts 21—26: Paul's arrest, trial, and various defenses before Felix, Festus, and Agrippa.

3. Christ will give His witnesses the words to say and the strength to do it. The sword of the Spirit will do mighty wonders in bringing many to faith. Look again especially at the Spirit's victories in Ephesus (**Acts 19:8-12, 17-20**).

4. Disciples will be betrayed by friends and relatives (**Acts 13:13:** John Mark deserts his uncle Barnabas and new friend, Saul).

Some will die as martyrs (**Acts 12:1-2:** James is executed).

Paul was hated by both Jew and Gentile (**Acts 14:8-20:** Both Jews and Gentiles have a hand in stoning Paul.)

5. Be on the alert to cite examples of where "called out-ones" suffer for their faith. Students may know of missionaries being killed by those they came to help. Don't overlook pastors and teachers who have given up lucrative careers in order to serve their Lord professionally. Untold thousands in communist countries are discriminated against because of their faith. In our own country a practicing believer who speaks up for Christ is sometimes excluded from social and economic advances.

2 Thess. 2:1-12

This takes us into the time before the end. That time may well be now.

1. **The "man of lawlessness"** will appear in the midst of rebellion, at a time when law and order are absent. Some will regard him as being more important than God. He will even invade the organized church and proclaim himself to be God (**vv. 3-4**).

He will also make use of seeming miracles that will deceive those who have already rejected the Gospel (**vv. 9-10**).

2. When Jesus returns **the "lawless one" will be revealed** and then promptly overthrown **"with the breath of His mouth" (v. 8).** This is another way of naming the sword of the Spirit (breath). The final battle will be waged on the basis of the truth of the Gospel: salvation through Christ.

3. The sword of the Spirit wins spiritual battles. It wins souls from the power of Satan. The church's battle is not to be a power, economic, or territorial struggle. History has shown how futile and embarrassing such power struggles have been when church leaders have tried to make Christ's kingdom an earthly one.

4. For this one be on the lookout for the many church appeals, ads, and campaigns to attract followers by any of the means listed. In some locations, these blurbs come to the attention of pastors and District officials.

If such ads or "blurbs" are not available, explain from your experience what goes on in such appeals. Don't leave this activity until the students are acquainted enough with each category to write an intelligent response.

The catagories listed below can be spotted by the following clues.

a. **Revealing the Future:** Many of the prophetic books are used to pinpoint actual battles, invasions, using actual countries. Israel, Russia, the United States, and England are often named.

b. **Working Miracles:** These are called miracle services where the lame, crippled, and bedridden are healed on the spot. Often healings are done en masse over the radio or by letter.

c. **Seeing Visions:** People from the

Bible, particularly Mary, appear in certain locations. Future events are sometimes predicted and sometimes healing occurs.

d. **Having Success in Life:** The message given is largely that if you have Jesus (note who owns whom) you will be blessed with success. Positive thinking, love, and kindness are the tools you need to obtain happiness.

e. **Learning Secrets:** These groups promise that they hold certain information that unlocks the meaning of life and success. Often these secrets reveal the future, and sometimes they hold the key to a healthy life.

SECOND HALF (Objective 4)

Allow time for this assignment. If there is enough interest, you might allow a day or two. At any rate, have these responses read and discussed in class. Above all, stress the need to show how salvation through Christ—and our access to life through faith—must never be compromised.

FINAL WHISTLE

Christ tells us to pray for those who persecute us and despitefully use us. Here would be a time to do it. Prayers for those who distort and misuse the Gospel are also in order.

Session 40: Within the Grasp of Victory

BIBLE BASIS: Phil. 3:12—4:1

CENTRAL TRUTH

Paul uses language of an athletic contest to describe our spiritual battle with Satan. Christ, who has won our victory for us, now calls and empowers us to finish the race and join Him in everlasting victory.

OBJECTIVES

That the students will

1. share ways to respond to Satan's attacks within congregations;

2. associate athletic training techniques with Paul's summary of our spiritual contest;

3. tell what this spiritual training program means in their lives.

BACKGROUND

This last session on our spiritual battle focuses on Paul's summary of it in Phil. 3:12—4:1. While not an athlete himself, Paul no doubt witnessed many Greek athletic events. He used this frame of reference to summarize our struggle with Satan's temptations.

Note the context of Paul's words. In **vv. 1–11** he emphasized that his goodness did not come from himself or the things he had done. (**"Whatever was to my profit I now consider loss for the sake of Christ"—v. 7**). No, Paul's righteousness **"comes from God and is by faith" (v. 9).** Be sure to stress that these truths also apply to us as we battle Satan today. We can be sure of victory—not because we are such valiant fighters, but because God gives us the victory.

The warm-up activity is the conclusion to session 39. Each student is to read his or her response to a false teaching found within organized congregations. This will lead into the Philippians text, where Paul summarizes his response. The final activity asks the students to reflect on their own life as Christ's warriors. The entire mood of this session should be upbeat inasmuch as we respond as warriors on the winning team.

Pray that the Gospel of Christ will make each of your students an effective warrior in the battle against Satan and his cohorts.

WARM-UP (Objective 1)

Have these responses read after a quick review of the attack as listed in session 39. As you listen and discuss, emphasize (1) the enthusiasm needed to recognize and go after an attack from Satan and (2) the power we have in this battle because God has made us His children. If students find fault with what others have written, remind them to do so in a spirit of meekness. Conclude this section with a prayer for guidance and strength.

FIRST HALF (Objective 2)

Devote most of this class session to **"Warm-Up"** and **"Second Half."** Spend just enough time with **"First Half"** to help students understand the analogy that Paul uses.

Make sure everyone understands the track and field techniques. Most of them are based on plain common sense. Number 5 might be somewhat technical. When a runner turns his or her head, the natural rhythm of stride and smooth arm action are broken. Psychologically, seeking the finish line is more positive than looking to see who might beat you.

Following are suggested verses:

1. 17.   4. 15–16.
2. 12.   5. 13–14.
3. 18–19.   6. 20–21.

SECOND HALF (Objective 3)

This activity becomes somewhat personal. The questions are intended to cause the students individually to examine their lives as warriors for Christ. To do this, allow some time for quiet, personal reflection. In some classes the responses could be shared within small discussion groups.

An excellent technique, but much more time-consuming, would be for you to individually talk with each student about his or her answers—in strictest confidence, of course. You would have to arrange for time outside of class or for some activity for the class to do while you confer with each student during class time.

Whatever you do, guard against pious "I can defeat the devil myself" or fatalist "I'm not match for him" responses. Through Jesus God gives us both power to fight in the battle and forgiveness for the times when we fail.

Phil. 3:12–14

1. Probably many entered God's kingdom in baptism, but others first received faith through the Word. Be on the lookout for any attempt to equate "being saved" with feeling a certain way. Conversion is entirely the work of the Holy Spirit.

2. This question provides an opportunity to emphasize the Gospel. Through Jesus we have both power and forgiveness.

3. We would not be able to be saved, since we do forget some sins and fail to recognize others. Our forgiveness does not depend on our remembering. Show how this is like "looking back" and getting out of the rhythm of Christ's forgiveness.

Phil. 3:15–16

Note that the question refers to differences in worship and expression of faith, and not to differences in faith. Our oneness with others occurs solely by God making things clear. The Spirit brings true unity. Even if we are of different backgrounds and expressions, we can still encourage one another in our Christian walk.

Phil. 3:17—4:1

1. Responses will vary. They may include such activities as Bible study, prayer, regular worship, personal witnessing, sharing, or one of the Ten Commandments.

2. Allow some speculation. Certainly we will be glorious (Phil. 3:21)! Phil. 4:1 indicates that we begin to receive that glory already now. We can already live the victorious life!

FINAL WHISTLE

Conclude the session with prayers of thanks for the assurance of victory. By now most or all students should be able to join in with a sentence or two.

Session 41: More than Conquerors

BIBLE BASIS: Rom. 8:28–39

CENTRAL TRUTH

St. Paul assures "called-out ones" that God has justified them. Therefore neither anyone nor anything will ever remove His love from them.

OBJECTIVES

That the students will

1. express confidence that God loves them and that Satan cannot change that;

2. identify God's five eternal acts on their behalf;

3. express belief that absolutely nothing will ever cause God to cease loving them and all people;

4. indicate that they are a part of the church and as such will also share in its victory.

BACKGROUND

With this session we begin a slightly different format. Since these last five sessions emphasize the victory that Christ has won for us, the session divisions will reflect this. The former "Warm-Up" will be called "Final Whistle," signifying the end of the contest and the beginning of the celebration. The sections formerly called "First" and "Second Half" will now simply be called "Celebration."

The follow-up activities usually found at the end of each session will appear in various locations. As usual, pick and use those that fit your class and situation.

Begin now to make plans for sessions 44 and 45. Session 44 will be a worship experience that will culminate the victory theme. Session 45 is a general review of unit 6. If you need to administer a final examination, be sure to begin now to prepare it. Also plan other ways, such as student interest and changes in behavior, to evaluate the course.

If you would ask a group of Christians to identify the Bible promise that means the most to them during a time of crisis, probably many would list **Rom. 8:28-39.** Young people, including high-school sophomores, may have trouble, however, comprehending the awesomeness of the message Paul presents here. Use whatever time is necessary to make this text come alive for them.

Pray that God will open the hearts of your students to this Gospel promise and that they will express to one another the assurance of the victory they receive from Him.

FINAL WHISTLE

Point out that athletic drills are merely means to an end, and that end is victory. We can speak all we want about "character building" and "having

fun," but if athletes seldom experience victory, they have little fun, and the character that is built is that of the loser.

How refreshing it is to be on the winning team! That is the message of Paul in **Rom. 8:28-39.** This text is one of the most uplifting in all of Paul's epistles.

CELEBRATION (Objectives 1-4)

Have one of your better readers read this text orally. Then have the students answer the questions individually. Be available, but don't immediately answer the questions. Lead students, but don't carry them.

The Gospel

1. *God* did not spare *God's* own Son, but gave *Christ* up for all *people*--how will *God* not also along with *Christ* graciously give us *people* all things?

2. Satan is the great accuser, even accusing God of being partial in **Job 1--2.** Satan tries to convince us that we are too bad to be loved and forgiven.

3. God declares us "not guilty." When Satan condemns us, we can be sure that Christ, who died for each of us, is at that moment pleading our case before God in heaven.

For "Called-Out Ones"

1. Paul refers to those who love Him as those "who have been called" according to His purpose.

2. These verses bring up the difficult topic of predestination. Do not get into the debate that if God predestines some to life, He must also then predestine some to death. The Bible does not say this. God provides this doctrine to strengthen the faith of the "called-out ones." We cannot determine the motives or methods of God. Paul is careful not to fall into this trap. See again **Eph. 1:3-10** for another treatment of this subject.

The five acts of God for us are
a. foreknew us   d. justified us
b. predestined us   e. glorified us.
c. called us

3-4. We in time are only able to experience the calling and justifying. But we can be just as sure of the three that occur in eternity.

As you discuss this activity, make sure that students understand that when Paul says that God "foreknew us," he was not just saying that God knew that we were good or that we would believe. God knew us *perfectly*, warts and all; He loved us in spite of them.

The puzzle will spell out:

F = foreknew
A = predestined
I = called
T = justified
H = glorified

This Is Sure!

1. **Verse 35 is the springboard into 37–39.** The ultimate answer is that nothing will ever remove God's love from us.

2 and 6. The list from **verses 38–39** might read:

a. death = Christ conquered it; made it a doorway to eternal life.

b. life = Christ transformed it to a glorious chance to demonstrate love.

c. angels = are confirmed as helpers for humanity.

d. demons = are restrained from thwarting God's plan.

e. present = no present day event can cancel out Christ's victory for us.

f. future = nothing in the future can undo what Christ did.

g. powers = are all subject to Christ, "King of kings; Lord of lords."

h. height = God's presence knows no boundary.

i. depth = No trouble is so bad that God cannot help.

j. anything else in all creation = everything God created is subject to Him.

3. Paul says that none of these can separate us from God's love.

4. The only item that Paul omitted is self. If separation occurs, God is not the one who moves. We, ourselves, are the only ones who can choose to leave God. Adam and Eve began the choosing of death in Eden. Humanity has continued. Christ has again put us in contact with God so, through the power of the Holy Spirit, we can accept His love. We can do this--and do it--because of God's gift of life to us.

5. Nothing!

6. Above in #2 we find possible responses to the reasons why the item listed cannot remove God's love. If you feel your class is not experienced enough to supply the reasons, suggest that they list the areas of their lives now or in the future that they feel might be a threat to their faith in God's love in Christ.

7. In the discussion time you might want to listen to the various concerns that surface. Using the list of reasons from #2 above, assure each student that God's love can overcome "anything in all creation."

8. Finally, discuss the last question. Paul always seems to thinks in terms of "we." Christ also used plural pronouns in the Lord's Prayer. As Christ's witnesses, "called-out ones" think in terms of love. Love always gives; it thinks of others first. God's grace is not to be selfishly hoarded; it is to be given away.

FINAL WORSHIP

Have the class read **Rom. 8:37–39** orally. Then pray the Lord's Prayer together.

Session 42: Swallowing Death

BIBLE BASIS: 2 Tim. 4:6–8

CENTRAL TRUTH

Both temporal and spiritual death have been defeated by Christ, who suffered separation from God on our behalf and absorbed the sting of death. He keeps His "called-out ones" faithful to Him and will raise us to life

eternal at the end of time.

OBJECTIVES

That the students will

1. explain that all believers must face death, but we may do so without fear, since it is the entrance to life;

2. explain the difference between spiritual and temporal death;

3. trace the effect that death has had on humanity and how Christ has defeated it;

4. be confident in the face of death because or their hope in Christ.

BACKGROUND

The topic of death may not be popular among teenagers, whose lives are just beginning. But death is, so to speak, a part of life. As "called-out conquerors," students should know that in spite of the world's attempts to hide it or ignore it, they can face it as the final step before their face-to-face reunion with Christ.

If the death of a loved one of someone in your class is still fresh in the minds of students, take advantage of that situation to personalize this lesson. Focus on the sure hope in Christ as presented in the Daniel and New Testament passages.

Pray that God will keep your students faithful until death, and that He will remove from their hearts the fear usually associated with death.

FINAL WHISTLE (Objective 1)

This fictional account is based on the tradition that St. Paul wrote his last epistle to Timothy around A.D. 66, after which he was executed under Nero. As recorded in **2 Tim. 4:11**, Luke was with Paul. According to Paul's previous practices, Luke no doubt wrote as Paul dictated.

Use this scene to show that not only sadness accompanies a Christian's death. Behind the sorrow of earthly separation we find the joy of a reunion with Christ in glory.

CELEBRATION (Objectives 1–4)

The Student Book does not get at the difference between *spiritual* and *temporal* death. Since these terms are not used in Scripture, it might be better for you to handle that topic directly.

Spiritual death is the separation of ourselves from God. It first occurred in **Gen. 3:8** when Adam and Eve tried to hide from God because of their sin. It is the natural state of humanity that requires the miracle of conversion by the Holy Spirit. *Spiritual death* results in eternal separation from God

in hell.

Temporal death is the separation of the body from life, first described by God in **Gen. 3:19**: **"to dust you will return."** It is the penalty for original sin and affects all people.

Christ's death for us changed both. On the cross He endured separation from His Father. Incredible as this is, it freed us from having to face an eternity in hell, because Christ did it for us. When Christ died, His body was separated from life, but he reversed the process by once again taking up His life into His body—the resurrection. We, too, will temporarily be separated from life, but will, as was He, be reunited with our bodies in the last resurrection.

Be sure students understand this concept before proceeding to the activities.

Christ Defeats Death

As you check the matching activity, be sure to encourage students to discuss the concepts presented. Then ask 12 students to read the 12 statements in sequence to reinforce the truths presented here. Try to develop both head knowledge and heart knowledge.

Following are the correct answers:

1.	d	7.	i
2.	e	8.	j
3.	f	9.	k
4.	g	10.	l
5.	h	11.	b
6.	a	12.	c

Facing Death Today

If the previous activity has generated many questions and led students to face death in a personal way, expressing confidence in a resurrection through Christ, you might omit this section.

An alternate approach would be to encourage students to ask questions that may be bothering them. Consider having them write their questions on a sheet of paper, turning them in anonymously. Answer questions honestly and forthrightly, if you can. If you can't, don't hesitate to say, "I don't know."

If you do have the students write the assigned topics, be sure to read and comment on them. Or have them read in class and provide time to discuss them. Try not to leave important questions unanswered.

Read 1 Cor. 15:50–58. Conclude with a student-led prayer of thanks for the victory over death.

Session 43: The Church at Home

BIBLE BASIS: Eph. 5:25–27;
Rev. 21:1—22:5

CENTRAL TRUTH
Christ's victory for His church entitles it to a new home, heaven. There God will provide glories and pleasures beyond human comprehension, the greatest of which will be the joy of being with Christ forever.

OBJECTIVES
That the students will
1. explain the Bride of Christ and the New Jerusalem analogies of the church;
2. translate the content of **Rev. 21:1—22:5** into real estate terminology;
3. express anticipation over the prospect of a life in heaven centered on being with Christ forever.

BACKGROUND
A look at the church in glory culminates the study of the church. St. Paul has little to say about the church triumphant, except for his analogy in **Ephesians**. We, therefore, venture into **Revelation** for a look into heaven. As stated in the Student Book, Scripture says little about heaven. **Ezek. 40—48** contains a parallel reading to the **Revelation** text. **Ezekiel** dwells more on symbolism based on Old Testament references. Emphasize the primary reason for being in heaven (to be with Christ) rather than focusing on our escape from a dreary and sinful earth.

One problem in reading **Revelation** is that of trying to identify and explain everything. The activities in this session are designed to whet the students' interest in the life to come, not to explain it. We use a real estate report to help students understand the Biblical account.

The items listed on that report are not exactly like those on a real

document. They have been "doctored" to fit the analogy. Use it to create some interest in what God has in store for us.

Work through the entire session together. The class will need your guidance both in reading **Revelation** and in the real estate document. As necessary, explain real estate terminology.

The climax of the activity comes at the end under **Terms.** Here you and your students can experience the Gospel in a different context.

Pray that the activities of this session will increase your students' desires to be with Christ forever in heaven, and that they will rely totally on His merits to achieve this goal.

FINAL WHISTLE (Objective 1)
Read through this introduction with the class, recalling from session 27 how the analogy of Christ and the church was used. Emphasize that we will focus on the church being Christ's bride. Make the transition to **Rev. 21—22,** where John refers to the church as the New Jerusalem, appearing as the bride of Christ.

Before reading **Rev. 21:1—22:5,** explain to the class that this is apocalyptic literature and as such is written in picture language. Not all details (such as the semiprecious stones of 21:19–21) need to be identified. Throughout the session emphasize the joy of being in God's presence, fulfilling His will and plan for us. Don't hesitate to say, "I don't know," or "We'll have to wait to find out" when necessary.

CELEBRATION (Objectives 2–3)
Work through this activity with your class. First read the text **(Rev. 21:1—22:5)** aloud once with little or no comment. Then work through each item on the questionnaire. Often you will need to explain the question

before the class begins to look for the answers. Allow some time for questions in connection with each item and additional discussion time to "pull it all together" after you have completed the questionnaire.

Persons and Property Involved

1. Agent: You as the instructor are a go-between. But the Holy Spirit is our most important Agent.

2. Prospective occupants: The church: "called-out ones" (21:27b).

3. Date of filing: Today's date. (Today is the day to hear and believe the Gospel.)

4. Date of possible occupancy: Day of death or Judgment Day, whichever comes first.

5. Name of dwelling: New Jerusalem, Holy City (21:2); "The Lord Is There" (Ezek. 48:35).

6. Location: a new heaven, a new earth (21:1); wherever God is, (21:3).

7. Age of structure: New (21:1).

8. Builder and developer: God (21:3; cf. Heb. 11:10).

9. Will owner live with occupant? Yes (21:3).

10. What environmental hazards will be excluded? Death, crying, pain, mourning (21:4); seas, feared by ancient people (21:1).

11. What individuals are excluded? Cowardly, unbelieving, vile, murderers, immoral, followers of magic, idolators, liars, etc. They are excluded because they reject God's grace. Therefore Christ's virtue does not fill their lives. Fruits of faith are absent.

Description of Property

1. Exterior apperance: Shines with glory of God, has a great high wall (21:11–12).

2. Number of doors: 12 gates (21:12). God often uses the number 12 to represent His people. It connects us with the 12 tribes of Israel and the 12 apostles.

3. Number and identification of foundations: 12 foundations, each named with one of the apostles (21:14). Refer to Eph. 2:20.

4. Measurements: Structure seems to be square: 12,000 x 12,000 x 12,000 stadia (21:15–16). 12,000 stadia may equal about 1,400 miles.

5. Construction material: Precious stones decorate the foundations, pearls form gates, and gold paves streets (21:18–21). Emphasis here is on the wealth beyond description that is our eternal inheritance.

Description of Amenities

1. Proximity of worship center: There is none. No temple is needed, since God is there and visible to all (21:22).

2. Lighting: No sun or moon. God Himself will provide light (21:22–25).

3. Water supply: The river and water of life coming from God's throne (22:1). See also Ezek. 47:1–10.

4. Vegetation and food availability: The Tree of Life, with fruit from this tree available every month (22:2). See Gen. 3:22–24 for more on the Tree of Life. Ezek. 47:12 also mentions the fruit of 22:2.

5. Medical facilities: The leaves of the tree are for healing the nations (22:2). The healing referred to here is obviously the spiritual healing of the rift between God and humanity.

Terms

This section provides an opportunity to summarize the Gospel message you have discussed during the course. Answers to all questions except 1 are based on the truths of God's Word as revealed throughout Scripture.

1. Terms of tenancy: Occupants will live and rule with God forever (22:5).

2. Asking price: Complete obedience to the Law. (Obviously too high, since occupants are unable to earn their own way.)

3. Selling price: The life of Jesus Christ, the Seller's own Son. Full payment made at Golgotha, Judea.

4. Down payment: The full selling price.

5. Monthly payments: None. Jesus has paid the account in full. (We could think of such things as remembering our baptism, hearing God's Word and partaking of the Lords' Supper regularly, and living a life that bears good fruit as some sort of vouchers, but none of them pays even in part for our life with Jesus in heaven. They are all means through which God comes to us or through which we respond in

love to the love He has shown to us.)

6. Name of buyer: The Triune God. Cf. **Acts 20:28b.**

7. Beneficiary: The church.

Invite volunteers to create newspaper adds from the above information.

Read **Rev. 22:12-17.** Choose three students to read one paragraph each. Have the class respond with **verse 20b:** "**Amen. Come, Lord Jesus.**" You conclude with **verse 21.**

Session 44: A Victory Party

BIBLE BASIS: Various readings from **Philippians, Revelation, Ephesians, and John**

CENTRAL TRUTH

God moves and empowers His young "called-out ones" to celebrate their joy in Christ's victory in worship by hearing and by responding with prayer, praise, and dedication.

OBJECTIVES

That the students will

1. experience the joy of worship, by hearing again the good news of Christ's victory;

2. express their willingness to use their lives in the service of Christ;

3. share the togetherness that comes from being members of the church.

BACKGROUND

Taking our cue from the previous session, we conclude with a great victory celebration. Young people like to party, but probably don't think of worship as a party. To dispel that notion, consider conducting this session as a party.

The Student Book says nothing about anything other than a worship experience. You may, however, decide to go beyond the suggestions there. Following are some possibilities:

1. Decorate the room with balloons, crepe paper streamers, and banners.

2. Plan some food for the latter part of the period.

3. Provide some games such as Bible Baseball, 20 Questions, or Bible Trivia for the latter part of the period.

4. These ideas can either be a surprise or you could enlist the help of the class to provide decorations, food, and games.

Pray that the celebration begun today may continue throughout the lives of your students and into eternity.

FINAL WHISTLE (Objective 2)

If you plan to do any of the above, the "**Final Whistle**" activity in the Student Book should be done outside of or before the class. Students are asked to make a statement about their desire to serve the Lord in the future. Some may not be ready or able to do this. They are also asked to say something about their feelings about each other. Again, this cannot be forced. Definitely, however, plan to have students read their statements of dedication as indicated in the outline.

To keep from forcing responses from those who do not feel so inclined, you might invite students to respond whenever they feel moved by the Spirit to do so. When no other students seem ready to respond, just go on with the next part of the worship, even if several have not participated verbally in this part.

CELEBRATION (Objectives 1-3)

If you wish, revise this outline to fit your situation. If possible, have the students sit in a circle facing each other. Choose readers ahead of time. Try to fit reading to individual ability and personality.

Following are suggestions for the various steps.

1. **Meditation:** Use time for writing, or if that was done, just quiet meditation.

2. **Invocation:** Change "Philippi" to the name of your class and school and "overseers and deacons" to "instructor and students."

3. **Hymn from Past:** Read as indicated.

4. **Hymns from Future:** Choose individuals to read as class follows in Bible.

5-6. Readings: Read by individuals with class responding as printed.

7. Sounds of Heaven:

a. Use a record or tape of "Hallelujah" or "Amen Chorus" from the *Messiah* by G. F. Handel. Or use another uplifting, stirring song of praise. Do not rule out having the class sing.

b. Have prepared statements read. If constructive comments develop--fine!

8. Circle Prayer: Have the class stand, hold hands, and use the usual procedure for a circle prayer.

9. The Our Father: Conclude circle prayer with this.

10. The Benediction: You should read this.

Depending on the class and situation, this worship can be a most meaningful experience, perhaps one they will not forget.

Session 45: Concluding Activities for Unit 6

Reread the comments on reviews found in session 10.

Use the questions that follow as a review, a test, or in another way that seems appropriate to you.

If you wish to construct an exam for the entire course, you might draw from the questions in the unit reviews. Be sure, though, to base the exam on material actually covered, including some of the activities and events that were unique to the course this time.

1. State in paragraph form the story of Satan's warfare with God through humanity.

(Satan was expelled from heaven, whereupon he stalks the earth seeking to take away the faith of believers. He succeeded in tempting Adam and Eve to sin. God, instead of consigning humanity to eternal punishment, promised to send a Messiah to redeem us and to defeat Satan. Christ was born, defeated Satan's temptations, and suffered and died for humanity's sins. Christ then rose from the dead and proclaimed His victory to Satan. He then assured His followers that they, too, will rise from the dead to live forever in glory.)

2. Name and describe the spiritual armor provided by God for each "called-out one."

(God provides the *belt of truth* to keep us free from misinformation that can lead to being unsure of God's love. The *helmet of salvation* keeps us conscious of being God's heirs and so keeps us headed straight. The *breastplate of righteousness* is the holiness that God clothes us with to protect us from Satan's accusations. The *shoes of the Gospel* provide us with

the motivation for moving into hostile territory. The *shield of faith* can be used to block nagging doubts and temptations that would surely leave us defenseless. The *sword of the Spirit*, our only offensive weapon, relies on God's Word to cut down Satan's temptations.)

3. Name the two edges of God's sword of the Spirit and what is to be done with each edge.

(The two edges of the Sword of the Spirit are *Law* and *Gospel*. The *Law* states what God wants us to do and shows that we haven't done it. The *Gospel* shows how God has kept the Law for us, paid our debt, and now makes us His own. The *Law* should be used to convict people of their sins. The *Gospel* should be used to assure the repentant that God, for Jesus' sake, has forgiven them.)

4. Name some of the devices Satan will use to try and deceive the nations.

(Satan has used and will use persecution, threats, desertion, betrayals, and even death to dissuade believers. In addition, he will use false teachers, miracles, promises of ease, peer pressure, visions, and other lies to tempt "called-out ones" to give up their faith.)

5. State six training and technique facts from track and field and tell how each can be compared to our struggle as "called-out ones."

(The six tract and field references are:

a. Keeping training rules--knowing and keeping the way Christ has set for us.

b. Daily practice in order to win--our

life should exercise our faith, knowing that we will win.

c. Breaking training rules hurts the team--sin hurts the entire body of Christ and gives a poor witness.

d. Give 100 percent all the time--God knows best how to use us; we therefore do all to His glory.

e. Never look back--keep eyes always on Christ and His goal for us. Looking back at a sinful life breaks our communication with Him.

f. Success comes from using your talents and from training--God has given us our abilities and He helps us use them to His glory.)

6. Name the five eternal acts of love that God has done for you as stated in **Rom. 8.** Explain each act, telling how it makes us more confident of our salvation.

(The five eternal acts of God are:

a. Foreknowing: God knows and loves us from eternity even though we are sinners.

b. Predestining: God planned beforehand that we would be a son or daughter by faith.

c. Calling: God works faith in our hearts through the Gospel.

d. Justifying: God declares us "not guilty" by virtue of Jesus' sacrifice for us.

e. Glorifying: God takes us from this life to live in eternity with Him.)

7. Tell briefly in one paragraph the story of how God through Jesus Christ has defeated death.

(The penalty for sin is that humanity would die spiritually in being separated from God and bodily by losing life. God promised that the Savior would defeat Satan and restore the original relationship between God and humanity. Nevertheless, people began to suffer the indignity of bodily death. When Christ died on the cross, He did that for all people, and when He rose from the dead He showed that bodily death is also defeated when all will rise from the dead. The final victory will be when all believers live

together with God in heaven forever.)

8. Describe in one paragraph what life will be like in heaven and tell the main reason for being there.

(The main reason we will be in heaven is to be with Jesus. Along with all "called-out ones," we will live in a new creation, where pain, suffering, and sin will be absent. God Himself will be the light and the center of our worship. He will provide for every need as we live with Him forever.)

9. Choose one song of victory from **Revelation** and tell why it is particularly meaningful to you.

(Answers will vary.)

10. After studying the church and your part in it, in what areas of your Christian faith have you grown?

(Answers will vary. This answer should reveal if factual input has been changed into more firm hold on the promises of Christ. It should also reveal if the students think in terms of "me" or "we.")

11. When you meet St. Paul in heaven, what will you talk to him about?

(Answers will vary. Notice if the subject of conversation is a question of Paul or a statement to him. Consider statements to be the product of a more mature outlook.)

12. Write a statement that sums up your belief concerning Jesus Christ and His importance in your life.

(Answers will vary. This question will lead to a subjective answer. And that is as it should be. After all, the faith of the church is the faith of each individual. As there are many different lively stones in God's temple, just so there will be that many different expressions of faith. But thank the Lord that in Christ we are all made one.)